The Complete Films *of*
Marilyn Monroe

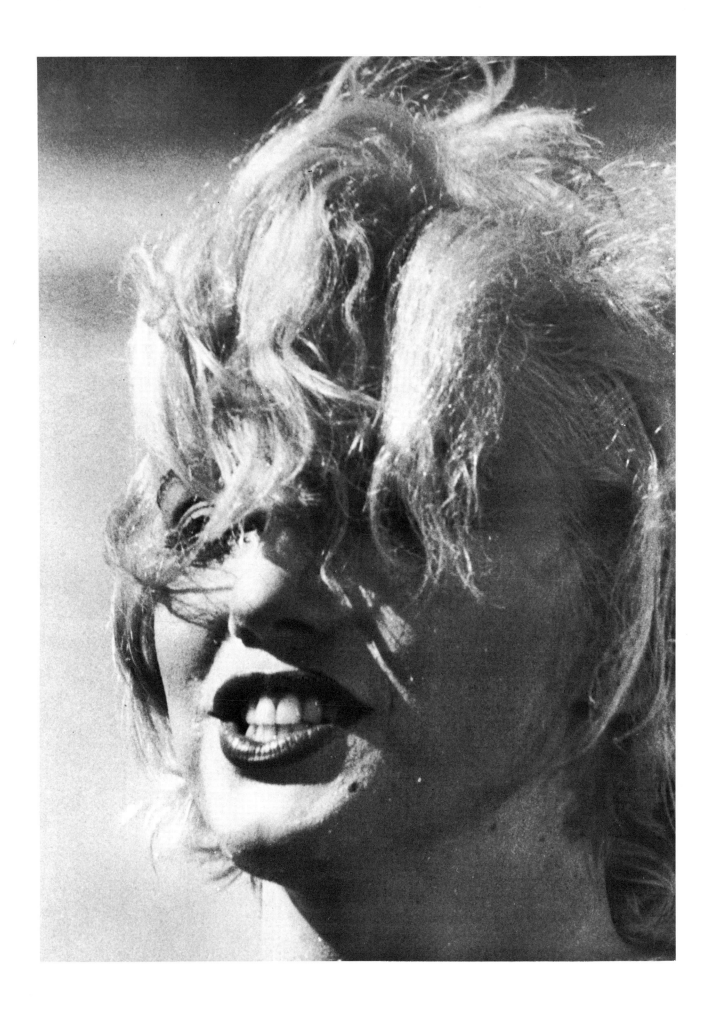

The Complete Films of Marilyn Monroe

By MICHAEL CONWAY and MARK RICCI

With a Tribute by Lee Strasberg
and an Introductory Essay by Mark Harris

A CITADEL PRESS BOOK   *Published by Carol Publishing Group*

First Carol Publishing Group Edition 1990

Copyright © 1964 by Michael Conway and Mark Ricci

A Citadel Press Book
Published by Carol Publishing Group

Editorial Offices	Sales & Distribution Offices
600 Madison Avenue	120 Enterprise Avenue
New York, NY 10022	Secaucus, NJ 07094

In Canada: Musson Book Company
A division of General Publishing Co. Limited
Don Mills, Ontario

Citadel Press a registered trademark of
Carol Communications, Inc.

Manufactured in the United States of America
ISBN 0-8065-1016-1

Carol Publishing Group books are available at special discounts
for bulk purchases, for sales promotions, fund raising, or
educational purposes. Special editions can also be created to
specifications. For details contact: Special Sales Department,
Carol Publishing Group, 120 Enterprise Ave., Secaucus, NJ 07094

12 11 10 9 8 7 6 5

Contents

A Tribute   7
Lee Strasberg

One American Woman: A Speculation Upon Disbelief   9
Mark Harris

Marilyn and Hollywood   17
Michael Conway

SCUDDA HOO! SCUDDA HAY!   23

DANGEROUS YEARS   24

LADIES OF THE CHORUS   26

LOVE HAPPY   31

A TICKET TO TOMAHAWK   35

THE ASPHALT JUNGLE   38

ALL ABOUT EVE   42

THE FIREBALL   46

RIGHT CROSS   48

HOMETOWN STORY   52

AS YOUNG AS YOU FEEL   57

LOVE NEST   60

LET'S MAKE IT LEGAL   65

CLASH BY NIGHT   68

WE'RE NOT MARRIED   72

DON'T BOTHER TO KNOCK   76

MONKEY BUSINESS   83

O. HENRY'S FULL HOUSE   89

NIAGARA   93

GENTLEMEN PREFER BLONDES   98

HOW TO MARRY A MILLIONAIRE   105

RIVER OF NO RETURN   110

THERE'S NO BUSINESS LIKE SHOW BUSINESS   116

THE SEVEN YEAR ITCH   122

BUS STOP   129

THE PRINCE AND THE SHOWGIRL   135

SOME LIKE IT HOT   141

LET'S MAKE LOVE   146

THE MISFITS   153

SOMETHING'S GOT TO GIVE   159

cA Tribute

Delivered by LEE STRASBERG, *artistic director*
of Actors Studio, at the funeral
of Marilyn Monroe, Thursday, August 9, 1962

Marilyn Monroe was a legend.

In her own lifetime she created a myth of what a poor girl from a deprived background could attain. For the entire world she became a symbol of the eternal feminine.

But I have no words to describe the myth and the legend. I did not know this Marilyn Monroe.

We, gathered here today, knew only Marilyn—a warm human being, impulsive and shy, sensitive and in fear of rejection, yet ever avid for life and reaching out for fulfillment. I will not insult the privacy of your memory of her—a privacy she sought and treasured—by trying to describe her whom you knew to you who knew her. In our memories of her she remains alive, not only a shadow on a screen or a glamorous personality.

For us Marilyn was a devoted and loyal friend, a colleague constantly reaching for perfection. We shared her pain and difficulties and some of her joys. She was a member of our family. It is difficult to accept the fact that her zest for life has been ended by this dreadful accident.

Despite the heights and brilliance she had attained on the screen, she was planning for the future; she was looking forward to participating in the many exciting things which she planned. In her eyes and in mine her career was just beginning. The dream of her talent, which she had nurtured as a child, was not a mirage. When she first came to me I was amazed at the startling sensitivity which she possessed and which had remained fresh and undimmed, struggling to express itself despite the life to which she had been subjected. Others were as physically beautiful as she was, but there was obviously something more in her, something that people saw and recognized in her performances and with which they identified. She had a luminous quality—a combination of wistfulness, radiance, yearning—to set her apart and yet make everyone wish to be part of it, to share in the childish naivete which was at once so shy and yet so vibrant.

This quality was even more evident when she was on the stage. I am truly sorry that the public who loved her did not have the opportunity to see her as we did, in many of the roles that foreshadowed what she would have become. Without a doubt she would have been one of the really great actresses of the stage.

Now it is all at an end. I hope that her death will stir sympathy and understanding for a sensitive artist and woman who brought joy and pleasure to the world.

I cannot say goodby. Marilyn never liked goodbys, but in the peculiar way she had of turning things around so that they faced reality—I will say au revoir. For the country to which she has gone, we must all some day visit.

One American Woman

A SPECULATION UPON DISBELIEF

by MARK HARRIS

Norma Jean Mortenson, known also as Norma Jean Baker, was born June 1, 1926, in or near Los Angeles under circumstances whose mysteries, after discommoding her childhood, would aggravate her mature anxieties. Of her father it was sometimes said that he died by automobile, sometimes that he died by motorcycle. Perhaps he was a baker. In any case, from the beginning he was effectively gone. The little girl dreamed of a father who looked like Clark Gable.

Of her mother more is known, but it is not encouraging. A film-cutter at R. K. O., she was reputed beautiful, but no claim was made for her peace of mind: betrayed and abandoned, penultimately widowed and finally insane, she in turn abandoned Norma Jean to a sequence of orphan-ages and foster homes. Norma Jean, who lost count, later estimated that she had lived with twelve families, each receiving, in those Depression days, $20 a month in public money for her care. Her first home, she re-called, was a "semi-rural semi-slum." She could turn a phrase.

Photographs show a lovely child, but the childhood wasn't. At the age of two she was almost smothered to death by an hysterical neighbor and at six almost raped by "a friend of the family." One family taught her to recite,

> I promise, God helping me, not to buy, drink, sell, or give.
> Alcoholic liquor while I live.
> From all tobaccos I'll abstain
> And never take God's name in vain,

but at the hearth of another her playthings were whiskey bottles.

At nine, in the Los Angeles Orphans' Home, her first big money was a nickel a month for pantry labor, of which a penny a Sunday went into the church basket. With the surplus penny she bought a hair ribbon. So runs the legend. She stuttered, she heard noises in her head, and she con-templated suicide.

At sixteen, working in a wartime aircraft plant, she was photographed by an Army publicity man who thought that the distribution of her picture among the fighting forces would serve an inspirational end. Indeed, one unit soon named her Miss Flamethrower, soldiers in the Aleutians voted her the girl most likely to thaw Alaska, and the Seventh Division Medical Corps elected her the girl they would most like to examine.

Then she married, perhaps to avoid being returned to an orphanage. She called him Daddy, and he called her Baby. For awhile they lived with his parents, later in "a little fold-up-bed place." It was a marriage which brought her, she afterward said, neither happiness nor pain, just an aimless silence. He entered military service. She modeled.

By the time of their divorce, in October, 1946, her face and figure had appeared upon several magazine covers and been seen by, among others, 20th Century-Fox, who signed her to a one-year contract at $125 a week and changed her name to Marilyn Monroe. A cameraman said, "Her natural beauty plus her inferiority complex give her a look of mystery."

She was twenty years old, and she must have believed, in her youth and relative innocence, that she was headed somewhere, like Up, like Success. She knew by her mirror that she was radiant, and she knew by her history that she had a nimble, preserving intelligence: Had she not thus far survived neglect, poverty, and a mistaken marriage? She thought, too, putting radiance and intelligence together, that she had a talent for acting. She studied acting at The Actors' Lab in Hollywood, literature at U. C. L. A. downtown, and lived frugally. She would afterward play in a moving picture called *How to Marry a Millionaire,* but in the life that was her own she was unmoved by millionaires. "I was never kept, to be blunt about it. I always kept myself. I have always had a pride in the fact that I was on my own." She owned 200 books (Schweitzer, Tolstoy, Emerson, Whitman, Rilke, Milton, Lincoln Steffens, and Arthur Miller) and records of Beethoven and Jelly Roll Morton.

It is not difficult to see, especially in retrospect, that she was uncommon, though to 20th Century-Fox, which paid a great many young ladies $125 a week, she was only one blonde girl in a world of blonde girls where even here or there an uncommon blonde was common enough. After a year, for lack of a clear motivation to renew, the studio allowed her contract to lapse.

Still she modeled. Once, for $50, she modeled anonymously nude on red velvet for a photographer named Tom Kelley, who was afterward proud of the fact that no matter how you turned the photograph its composition was impeccably symmetrical. The photograph, turned calendar, brought him $900 from a printer who sold it in quantity for three-quarters of a million dollars to barber shops, gasoline stations, ships' galleys and soldiers' barracks wherever men mark time across the world. Several years later, when her proprietors feared that the revelation of the calendar would damage her career, she refused to disclaim it. "Sure I posed. I was hungry." As a child she had had persistent dreams of walking naked in church over the prostrate forms of her friends, neighbors, and foster parents, "being careful not to step on anyone."

In 1950, in a pair of lounging pajamas, she played a small part in a motion picture called *The Asphalt Jungle.* She had auditioned for the director, John Huston. "I remember she was nervous," Huston remembered. "But she knew what she wanted. She insisted on reading for the role sprawled on the floor. She wasn't satisfied. She asked if she could do it again. But she had the part the first time . . ." Joseph Mankiewicz, watching her in *The Asphalt Jungle*, wanted her for a picture called *All About Eve*, and Zanuck, watching her in *All About Eve*, reclaimed her for 20th Century-Fox, this time with a seven-year contract beginning at $500 a week.

So much money resounds with authority. But it was less than star money, and Hollywood above all is stars—names and faces capable of magically drawing the public into movie-houses in spite of the force of such competing attractions as television, bowling, motoring, and bed-rest. Miss Monroe was not yet a star.

Of course, she was soon to become one, and she must have believed, at twenty-five years and $500 a week, that the choices and decisions of her life had thus far been more right than wrong. Almost everything her culture had ever taught her, and all that she had ever known or seen or heard, must have impressed upon her mind the American fact that More is Up; Success. Or even if she doubted this, alone of an evening with Schweitzer or Tolstoy (she took little pleasure in night-life; felt no necessity to be seen), who in Hollywood could possibly have corroborated or encouraged her skepticism, or explored its implications with her, or really seriously persuaded her or anyone that the shape of death might early appear even in the indisputably happy form of a moving-picture invitingly entitled *Don't Bother to Knock*, which grossed $26,000 in its first week in New York in spite of bad movie-going weather and bad newspaper reviews?

The pictures *Niagara* and *Gentlemen Prefer Blondes* quickly followed. In the first she showered in silhouette, in the latter she danced *á la* burlesque, bumps and grinds pruriently denatured to satisfy a code which, forbidding nakedness, provides the basic material from which interested persons may labor independently upon their own fantasies. (American culture, Isaac Rosenfeld has written, "is contradictory with respect to sex, urging its members on in a riot of stimulation, while it upholds conventional and moral restraints and taboos.")

For Marilyn Monroe a formula had been found. Henceforth she would be compelled to perform according to the formula so long as the profit flowed. The very titles of the moving-pictures with which she was associated during the early 1950's suggest the restrictions of that formula— *Ladies of the Chorus, Love Happy, Let's Make it Legal, Love Nest*.

By 1954 she was a star. In that year she made *The Seven-Year Itch*, and after the shooting attended a supper in her honor, arriving an hour late in a red chiffon gown borrowed from the studio. She had never owned an evening gown. Now for the first time she met Clark Gable, once the fantasy father of the fatherless child. She was twenty-eight years old, and she danced in his arms.

How is 20th Century-Fox like a little girl in a borrowed blue sweater?

In West Los Angeles, when Norma Jean was twelve years old, she went to school one day in a borrowed blue sweater. The boys of her class "suddenly began screaming and groaning and throwing themselves on the floor." After school they went to her house. "For the first time in my life I had friends. I prayed that they wouldn't go away." But an even more effective way to keep them was to wear the blue sweater again. This she learned.

Marilyn Monroe and 20th Century-Fox produced happiness by formula. For several years they were very happy together. In a decade of crisis in Hollywood she was one answer to the single question the industry asked: What sells? It no longer even pretended to be art or even serious. The question once was asked, "Who reads an American book?" Now one might ask, "Who sees an American movie?" Its principal function had become its exclusive function—to respect the ultimate consumer's sacred whimsy. What's good for Hollywood is good for the U. S. A. Profit and democracy are sisters under the skin.

In our early years we learn to produce happiness by formula. But what do we do when what we've become disgusts us and fills us with self-contempt?

The course of Marilyn Monroe's career had received its first impetus from the old penchant of large numbers of men for photographs—pin-ups—to be hung upon walls for the purpose of study. If claim may pass as fact, Miss Monroe, by the end of 1951, hung upon more walls than any other American woman; 20th Century-Fox was soon receiving, says one report, "thousands of letters a month" requesting her photograph.

Why Marilyn Monroe? Few of her admirers had ever seen her act in a movie, and to most of them her name was unknown. Why not any of a hundred or a thousand young ladies who had contrived to appear upon the cover of a magazine?

My first inclination is to search for publicity machinery behind a phenomenon so irrational. But no, whatever it was, Miss Monroe had it. It was hers. It came through. It was felt. It defied imitation, like the syrup of Coca-Cola. And her very namelessness may have been chief among her charms.

Was this not the simplest and purest and least menacing relationship most of her admirers had known? Perfectly sexual, she was also absolutely silent. So long as she was only a picture on the wall she could never outwit nor outsmart her partner, while, like the paper doll of the song, she was always waiting, she could never be stolen. A relationship with her was therefore effortless, without mess or obligation, totally uncomplicated. Above all, she provided that highest of all selfish pleasure, for she demanded no equality of pleasure, no exchange, no collaboration, no mutuality.

In the film *The Seven-Year Itch* the pin-up turned to flesh. Marilyn Monroe played The Girl upstairs whom Tom Ewell downstairs more or less hopes to seduce while his wife's away. But he doesn't really dare, or can't, or won't. Like the red-blooded Americans peeping at pin-ups in gas stations and ships' galleys, he can't relate with sufficient grace to a live and superior beauty. Such a relationship would force him to grant all her humanity, as if he believed not only in her tape-measure dimensions (finally paper-thin for safety's sake) but in the dimensions of her mind and her spirit.

As the success of her formula increasingly bored her, Marilyn Monroe more and more expressed her desire to become an actress, thus to employ the larger range of her womanhood. This desire was generally viewed as amusing but impractical. *Life* magazine called this ambition "irrational," and *Time* said that "her acting talents, if any, run a needless second" to her truest virtues—"her moist 'come-on' look . . . moist, half-closed eyes and moist, half-opened mouth." The journalists, incapable of believing in motivations not their own—believing in fame and gross receipts and the easiest popular expectations of women—could never imagine what more Miss Monroe might have wished to be. Didn't she, after all, fulfill *their* idea of a woman? "You know, journalists," said Arthur Miller—the playwright, her third husband—"usually come around with an angle. They *have* to. They simply never get the time or the opportunity to hang around long enough to decide anything. Over the years that angle becomes the easiest thing to do."

Above all, the danger lies in the thinking that makes it so. Sufficiently propagandized, the innocent believes in his guilt, as Marilyn Monroe learned to believe in her limitations, and as women in general perhaps do. Of course we freely say, "I don't care what anybody thinks," but of course we care. At the time of her marriage to Joe DiMaggio in 1954 she must herself have capitulated to a public image of herself which had overwhelmed her private conviction. His life was his body, his power was his power. It must have seemed to her a proper wedding because a proper definition of herself. Within a year it ended. Mrs. Joe DiMaggio she wasn't. That she knew. Nor The Girl upstairs. Nor a pin-up. At this time of her life, said a friend, she was engaged in "an absolute desperate attempt to find out what she was and what she wanted."

One thing she didn't want was 20th Century-Fox's film, *How to be Very Very Popular*. She walked out, announcing the formation of an independent company to be known as Marilyn Monroe Productions, Inc. More money? Perhaps so. But she had been "drowning in Hollywood" (Eli Wallach's phrase) and she was determined, he said, not to spend the rest of her life "just wiggling [her] behind."

"I want to expand," said Miss Monroe, "to get into other fields, to broaden my scope. . . . People have scope, you know, they *really* do." She declared herself, at this time, with a remark which was to plague her. She said, "I want to play strong dramatic parts, like Grushenka," an assertion which was to be hurled mockingly back at her, quite as if her experiences as waif and queen among peasants and lechers rich and poor in Southern California necessarily deprived her of a Dostoievskian outlook.

Hollywood minimized her by laughing at her. Director Billy Wilder, cynically reducing her new hope to the old focus, cheerfully said he would be pleased to direct her not only in *The Brothers Karamazov* but in a series of *Karamazov* sequels, such as *The Brothers Karamazov Meet Abbott and Costello, etc.* Disputing her claim that she needed training in acting, Wilder expressed in a breath the ruling conviction of both commercial Hollywood and an America gaping at pin-ups: "God gave her everything. The first day a photographer took a picture of her she was a genius." Her employer summed it up more formally. "20th Century-Fox," said 20th Century-Fox, "is very satisfied with both the artistic and financial results from the pictures in which Miss Monroe has appeared."

For a year, in New York, she led a private life. She studied acting with Lee and Paula Strasberg at The Actors Studio. I say *studied*, implying teachers, though I suspect that the Strasbergs served mainly as counselors, cheerleaders, psychologists whose talk was perhaps less instruction than a demonstration of faith. All teachers of adults have had the experience of the woman touching thirty who has come to realize that she has for some time known what exists to be known, but who needs an outer voice to confirm the inner. "For the first time I felt accepted, not as a freak, but as myself." Praised for her acting, her health improved. Here her circle of friends also included Arthur Miller.

Miller's interior, like hers, baffled the press. The marriage of Miller and Miss Monroe was described by one reporter as "the most unlikely . . . since the Owl and the Pussycat"—the familiar insistence, in the language of American disbelief, upon the imagined incongruity between brains and beauty, love and intellect, flesh and sensibility. Owning no matching veil for her beige wedding dress, she dyed one in coffee. The groom, though he was wealthy enough, owned only two suits—"the one he was married in," the bride said, "and the other one." Miller posed for photographers awkwardly, perhaps because grudgingly, resisting the insolence of the expectation that a man married to Marilyn Monroe must necessarily embrace her during every waking moment. Nor did Miller ever answer the question most often asked by obsessed reporters, "What does Marilyn wear to bed?" On the back of a wedding picture the bride wrote, "Hope, Hope, Hope."

He spoke of her always as actress, person; as mind, never as freak. Of her acting he said, "I took her as a serious actress before I ever met her. I think she's an adroit comedienne, but I also think that she might turn into the greatest tragic actress that can be imagined." His own arduous habits of labor enabled him to share her distress at moments when others viewed her as merely petulant. "In a whole picture," he said, "there may be only two scenes of which she is really proud. She has great respect for the idea of acting, so great that some part of her is always put to shame by the distance between what she achieves and the goal she has set for herself."

It was a noble strategy and a clearheaded loyalty, too late. Nor is it irrelevant that at the time of their marriage Miller's dispute with the Congressional un-American Activities Committee centered about the question of loyalty—his refusal to implicate associates of his political past. "The only real territory left," he said in another connection, "is relationship to other people. There really never was any other territory. . . ."

Miller said once, "Marilyn identifies powerfully with all living things, but her extraordinary embrace of life is intermingled with great sadness." This conception of her he carried into a short story, *Please Don't Kill Anything,* in which a girl with a "startling shape" laments fish dying upon a beach. She wants to throw them back. Her less anguished escort—her husband—points out that there are twenty-five miles of beach alive with dying fish. "He did not bend to pick them up because she seemed prepared to sacrifice them and he went back to her, feeling, somehow, that if he let those two die on the beach she might come to terms with this kind of waste." Once, during her first marriage, she had tried to bring a cow indoors out of the rain; as Rosalyn, in Miller's screenplay *The Misfits,* she would oppose the killing of horses.

In the autumn of 1956 the Millers went to England, where she made *The Prince and the Showgirl* with Laurence Olivier—another "unlikely" match, said the very magazine (*Life*) with the very word it had used to describe her marriage to Miller. The British newspapermen asked her what she wore to bed.

The picture was made, though not without friction among the principals. When it was done Miss Monroe apologized to the acting company for having been "so beastly," writing: "I hope you will all forgive me. It wasn't my fault. I've been very sick all through the picture. Please, please don't hold it against me." To some commentators such a note, from a lady so wealthy, so famous, so well-married, and with so little apparent reason to be difficult, had a whining sound.

Two miscarriages and gynecological surgery during the months that followed were perhaps more convincing. There were also two pictures—a lively comedy called *Some Like It Hot;* and *Let's Make Love,* with Yves Montand, whose expressions of admiration for her "professional conscience" tended to be lost among newspaper rumors that he and she were in love.

In Nevada, in the summer of 1960, she began *The Misfits.* It would be her last film. It was also Clark Gable's last film. In September her exhaustion forced an interruption, but the work was soon resumed and completed. The following February, divorced from Miller, she entered a clinic in New York for rest and psychiatric treatment. Fourteen months later she began work upon a film called *Something's Got to Give,* but she answered less than half her calls, and the shooting schedule fell impossibly behind. "She was sick, she insisted," according to *Life.* "She was reneging on her contract, said 20th Century-Fox. . . . Fox blew the whistle. They fired the star and filed a $750,000 lawsuit against her. . . ." To the cast and crew she had wired a message echoing her message to the company of *The Prince and the Showgirl* six years before: "Please believe me, it was not my doing . . . I so looked forward to working with you." Four months later she was found dead in her bed.

Whatever it was that worked its poisons upon her—three dead marriages, two miscarriages, an absent father, an insane mother, a forlorn childhood, a devouring press, the revelations of psychiatry—disbelief in herself was an obvious fact and perhaps a first factor. It so deeply undercut her belief in her own potentiality that she was equally unable to believe in Miller's belief in her. Who was Arthur Miller that he knew more than the whole world knew? "You know, journalists," said Arthur Miller. "Over the years that angle becomes the easiest thing to do, and it's gotten, in Marilyn's case, to be very fruitful in terms of copy. And they keep pounding her all the time until that thing becomes reality. By that time, it's impossible to imagine anything else."

First reports of the death of Marilyn Monroe said she died nude, later reports corrected the first, and a panting world knew at last what Marilyn Monroe wore to bed. But would anybody believe her, even now? "It can't be, it can't be," cried a Hollywood agent, "she couldn't have killed herself, she had three deals going."

Marilyn and Hollywood

by MICHAEL CONWAY

The war was over, peace reigned supreme, and Marilyn Monroe was signed to a contract by Twentieth Century-Fox. The year was 1946. Marilyn was young, pretty and hopeful, but, alas, she was one player among many under contract.

At this time, Betty Grable was Fox's glamour queen. She had been Hollywood's pin-up favorite during the war and now, with such pictures as "Mother Wore Tights," she was at the height of her popularity, America's symbol of wholesome sex. She had that rare combination of sexual attractiveness and girl-next-door appeal which few other actresses could convey across the movie screen. Marilyn Monroe's screen image could never have been the same. The public had just settled down to normalcy after a long and bitter war and was not ready for a "blonde bombshell" the likes of Marilyn. Apparently, neither was Twentieth Century-Fox. After being edited out of one film and playing a small role in another, she was dropped by the studio.

Marilyn was signed by Columbia for the second girl lead in "Ladies of the Chorus," a very tame movie about burlesque. Films about burlesque *had* to be tame in 1948 to be accepted by theaters. Marilyn, however, did manage to make her unique brand of sex appeal light up the screen in her musical number. That ability to convey raw sex combined with innocence, which was Marilyn's greatest asset in her climb to stardom, was very much in evidence in this film.

When Columbia also dropped her after this one film appearance for them, Marilyn might have given up in her attempt to make the big time, but her determination never wavered. Prospects were slim. Although there were many "blonde" featured parts available, there were also many blondes to fill them. Finally, Marilyn did get such parts. The Marx Brothers hired her for a walk-on in "Love Happy," which also was the last film for the three funny men as a team. Then in "Ticket to Tomahawk" she was in several scenes but had no lines. However, the latter film showed that she was changing from a pretty girl into a beautiful woman.

By 1950, that arch-enemy of the silver screen, television, was causing the movie studios to make an agonizing reappraisal of themselves. Entertainment provided on the home screens eventually caused the major studios to eliminate low-budget films from their production schedules. Not only were many of these inexpensive films of high quality but they also gave the studios a chance to show off promising players to the public. With their disappearance, studios stopped placing many young people under contract. Only the most magnetic could hope to achieve anything approximating stardom.

The studios also began to produce more realistic films which came to be called "adult" (a term often misused). Nevertheless, it was such a film that brought Marilyn Monroe her first recognition. "The Asphalt Jungle," directed by John Huston, was a grim, hard, honest film; it called for the type of cast which could be completely integrated into the plot no one person singled out as the star. Marilyn accommodated herself to this formula, contributing a fine performance without overshadowing Louis Calhern, who appeared with her in every one of her scenes. Although she wasn't singled out by critics, she was mentioned by them. The public also noticed her for the first time. It is quite likely that had she not appeared in this film, she might never have achieved stardom.

Marilyn got another break when she was cast in a small but choice role in Darryl F. Zanuck's "All About Eve." The sparkling dialogue written by Joseph L. Mankiewicz, who also directed this film, gave her a chance to show that she could handle other roles as well as she had the part of the slinky mistress in "The Asphalt Jungle."

Marilyn's next few roles ranged from featured parts in "The Fireball" and "Home Town Story" to a bit in "Right Cross." She was not a star, but she was getting work.

After thinking it over, Fox signed her to a contract on the basis of her performance in "All About Eve." The studio was, quite realistically, concerned about Marilyn's acting ability. She had done well in supporting roles but they were not sure that she could handle a starring role. Television had taken away a substantial part of the motion picture audience and starring Marilyn immediately in a film might have resulted in financial disaster. The studio assigned her parts in which she could be shown off but in which she had no responsibility for carrying the picture. These were the "blonde" roles she did so well. "As Young As You Feel," "Love Nest," and "Let's Make It Legal" were her first three films under the new contract. The starlet got her share of critical notice in reviews of these films. Perhaps it was only a line or so, but at least she wasn't ignored.

Bosley Crowther, motion picture critic for the *New York Times,* in his review of "As Young As You Feel," said that Marilyn was superb as the secretary. Mr. Crowther did not use this adjective often in reviewing Marilyn's subsequent performances. He, as well as other critics, alternated praise with censure. Marilyn needed this type of criticism whether she liked it or not. It was the only way she could measure her growth as an actress.

Fox loaned her to Wald-Krasna for "Clash By Night," which was released by the RKO Radio studio. It was the public's reaction to her performance in this film that made Fox really Monroe-conscious. She handled herself admirably, co-starring with three seasoned professionals.

Meanwhile, our society was becoming transformed. A new frankness about sex was emerging. Marilyn became the sex goddess of the new era, giving the movie industry the kind of boost it needed to answer the challenge of television. No screen personality in years had obtained such a huge following.

After a role in the delightfully saucy "We're Not Married," Fox gave Marilyn a difficult dramatic part in "Don't Bother to Knock," the film in which Marilyn played a mentally disturbed baby sitter. She did rather well considering her lack of experience with this type of role. The majority of adverse criticism centered on the dazed and dreamy manner she gave the psychotic girl. Since the girl of the story lived in a world of fantasy, it might be argued that such a manner was in character.

Marilyn's next film, "Monkey Business," concerned a man rejuvenated by a chemical mixture. Fox felt that comedy was Marilyn's forte and that she was not ready for another "Don't Bother to Knock" type of part. Besides, the public loved her in comedy roles.

Despite the many jokes about the unread books she carried, Marilyn was becoming a comedienne of the first rank. There were many blondes around trying to imitate her style. None of them succeeded. Apparently she did read some of those books.

Her role in "O. Henry's Full House" was small, but by now, any film with Marilyn was bound to make more money than it would have without her.

Fox now realized that they had the hottest property in Hollywood in their possession. The public wanted more and more Marilyn Monroe. Fox not only gave them Marilyn in her first starring role but also Niagara Falls in the film "Niagara." Now if anyone believed that watching someone walk was the dullest thing in the world, he had to change his mind. Marilyn's long walk in a tight red dress clearly exposed the character of the woman she was playing. She made the wanton wife in the film so evil that the audience almost rejoiced when she was murdered by the husband she was trying to drive insane.

After "Niagara" it was a foregone conclusion that Marilyn would never be anything but a star. Her next film, "Gentlemen Prefer Blondes," saw her co-starring with RKO Radio's glamour queen, Jane Russell. They must have become friends during the filming, because they worked together in perfect harmony. This type of accord cannot be induced even by the greatest of directors. When the movie was shown on television for the first time, Miss Russell spoke warmly about Marilyn. Although both were sex symbols, they each had more depth of character than comes across on the screen. There is danger when people confuse the symbol with the person. This may have been one of the reasons for the tragedy that followed almost a decade later.

"How to Marry a Millionaire" was released shortly after "Gentlemen Prefer Blondes." Marilyn was now co-starred with Fox's biggest glamour girl, Betty Grable. Betty must have known that the studio was grooming Marilyn as their top star, but no newspaper accounts of the filming of this movie contain any hint of friction between the two. They even seem to have been friends. This film was as successful as the two that had preceded it. Marilyn knew comedy and its various nuances.

The western, it seems, has become a must for every Hollywood star. Marilyn was no exception, hers being "River of No Return." Except for a

saloon sequence, Marilyn wore blue jeans, and in this garb was more alluring than many a richly costumed heroine typical of the genre.

Marilyn had proved that she could deliver a song well in "Gentlemen
Prefer Blondes." When she was cast in the musical extravaganza, "There's
No Business Like Show Business," she was given three musical numbers to
do. This was her major contribution to the film and she decided to do it
her way. One song especially, "Heat Wave," was criticized. Reviewers of
the film were divided in their reaction to her delivery, but the dissenters had
never been more acid. Why Marilyn did the numbers in such a sensual way
has been the subject of much speculation.

Marilyn's marriage to Yankee baseball star Joe DiMaggio ended during
the filming of her next movie, "The Seven Year Itch." Many feel her
portrayal of The Girl in this film was lifelike because she played it straight
as a not-too-bright blonde. This is debatable. It seemed apparent to this
viewer that she was throughout perfectly aware of what the character
played by Tom Ewell was all about. The Girl, as Marilyn saw and played
her, recognized that Sherman was going through a kind of crisis. This is
underlined at the end of the picture in the sisterly kiss she gives him as he
rushes to join his wife.

"Bus Stop," the star's next vehicle, saw her in the best performance of
her career. Kim Stanley, an outstanding actress, had played the role of
Cherie on the Broadway stage. Everyone wanted to see how Marilyn would
handle the role, the strongest she ever had, on the screen. Whether it was
due to Joshua Logan's direction, her study at the Actors Studio, or her own
innate ability, her performance in "Bus Stop" showed that she could do
herself proud in a role that required skill and subtlety.

Now whenever anyone mentioned the name Marilyn, it was assumed he
meant Monroe. She had made the word "movie" mean something special
at a time when people were generally addicted to the still-novel television
screen. Meanwhile, she was trying to change her screen image. Her rebellion
against assigned roles is illustrated in the wish she expressed to play the
part of Grushenka in "The Brothers Karamazov." Grushenka is indeed a
fascinating character—few would deny that—but not one easily transferred
to film. In any case, this avowed ambition is indicative of the star's changing
attitude toward her work.

Hollywood was also undergoing a change greater than the change of the
early fifties. Television and high production costs had caused RKO Radio
and Republic studios to close down production. Major studios were financing independent producers who in turn were releasing their films through
the financing studio. It was quite evident that the independent producer
was becoming the most important person in films. Marilyn decided to
become a producer. She set up her own company and bought the rights to
"The Sleeping Prince." For producers or directors to set up their own com-
panies was not as big a risk as it was for a performer. But Marilyn was such
sure boxoffice that she felt her company was bound to prosper. "The Sleeping Prince" was retitled "The Prince and the Showgirl" and was filmed in
England with Laurence Olivier directing as well as co-starring. Olivier
wisely let Marilyn have the best of it during their scenes together.

Marilyn was now married to Arthur Miller, the playwright. She may
have been trying to play too many roles. Star, wife, businesswoman. It

appears that she was not as enthusiastic about having her own company as time went on as she had been when she started the whole thing.

Director Billy Wilder persuaded Marilyn to appear in his comedy, "Some Like It Hot." It was a risky type of comedy because it involved transvestitism, although the principals engaged in it in self-defense in the story. Actually, though a broad farce, the film was done in the best of taste and no problem arose because of its theme. Although Marilyn enhanced it greatly, the movie belonged to Jack Lemmon and Tony Curtis. It became one of the most successful and profitable films ever made.

It was said that Marilyn felt her power during the last few years and that her attitude toward people she worked with caused many disputes. It is possible that had she remained a blonde featured player, she might have been a happier person. She had always been suspicious of people's motives. A wretched childhood still haunted her and her climb to stardom had not been easy. It is hard, however, to see a star as an underdog, and many felt that she abused the prerogatives of her position.

Marilyn returned to Fox and appeared in a light comedy called "Let's Make Love." It was destined to be her last film for this studio. Her next vehicle was "The Misfits" by Arthur Miller, in which she co-starred with Clark Gable. It was the last film for both. "The Misfits" demonstrated that Marilyn could handle a dramatic role with finesse. Indeed, it is clear that she could have carved out a new career for herself in dramatic roles.

Whatever troubled this sad woman is not for this writer to say. Everything was happening fast now. Soon after her marriage to Miller broke up, Fox assigned her to work in a new film, "Something's Got to Give," but her appearances on the set were so infrequent that the studio managed to get only a few minutes of her on film. Finally, the studio suspended her, announcing that shooting would resume with a replacement.

Marilyn was found dead on August 5, 1962, in her home at Brentwood, California. Cause of death was an overdose of barbiturates—and perhaps too much success and too little happiness.

What makes motion pictures unique is that they survive time. As long as there are movie projectors, future generations will be able to see this brilliant artist who in private life progressed from sad girl to sad woman; a girl who was truly an American Phenomenon.

The Films
of
Marilyn
Monroe

With Robert Karnes and Colleen Townsend

Scudda Hoo! Scudda Hay!

A Twentieth Century-Fox Picture (1948)

When Marilyn Monroe got her first contract with Twentieth Century-Fox she was cast in this picture in the bit role of a farm girl. The stars were June Haver and Lon McCallister, McCallister playing the role of a farm boy who successfully trains a pair of mules that no one else can handle; June Haver the part of a farm girl in love with McCallister.

Photographed in Technicolor, the film would have shown off Marilyn's youthful beauty had not her scenes wound up on the cutting room floor. Although this cannot properly be counted as one of her films, a photo with Marilyn in it is essential to a book on her film roles. If you see this film, watch for a scene at a lake with young people swimming. Look at the lake and you will see in the distance two girls rowing in a canoe. They are Marilyn and Miss Townsend, but their faces cannot be seen.

With William Halop

Dangerous Years

A Twentieth Century-Fox Release (1948)

CAST

William Halop, Ann E. Todd, Jerome Cowan, Anabel Shaw, Richard Gaines, Scotty Beckett, Darryl Hickman, Harry Shannon, Dickie Moore, Donald Curtis, Harry Harvey, Jr., Gil Stratton, Jr., Joseph Vitale, Marilyn Monroe, Nana Bryant.

CREDITS

Produced by Sol M. Wurtzel. Associate producer, Howard Sheehan. Directed by Arthur Pierson. Story and screen play by Arnold Belgard. Photography by Benjamin Kline. Musical score by Rudy Schrager. Edited by Frank Balridge.

SYNOPSIS

Jeff Carter (Donald Curtis) has succeeded in halting delinquency among teenagers in his town with the help of a boys' club. However, a young hoodlum named Danny Jones (William Halop) arrives on the scene and becomes friendly with the teenagers. Doris Martin (Ann E. Todd), Willy Miller (Scotty Beckett) and Leo Emerson (Darryl Hickman) are among those who come under his influence. (Marilyn Monroe has the role of a waitress named Eve at a juke box joint where the teenagers hang out.)

Leo cannot go through with a robbery planned by Danny, and tells Carter. When Carter tries to stop Danny, Danny kills him. Danny is arrested and brought to trial.

During the trial, Danny's lawyer, Weston (Jerome Cowan), describes the youth's early life in an orphanage. Connie, the daughter of District Attorney Burns (Richard Gaines), had been reared in the same orphanage. It is brought out that Connie had been born after her parents' separation and was later placed in the orphanage. A nurse told Burns that his child was in the orphanage and he took Connie out to raise at home. He had been previously unaware of the child's existence.

When the nurse sees that Danny is on trial, she tells him privately that he is actually Burns's son, confessing that she had identified Connie as Burns's daughter because Connie was sick and she had hoped that Burns would help to restore the child's health if he thought she was his. Danny swears the nurse to secrecy.

Danny is convicted and sentenced to prison, taking his secret with him.

This first role of Marilyn's was a bit, to be sure, but it was a start. However, Fox was to drop her contract before anything more substantial could come her way. The film had been produced independently by Sol M. Wurtzel, who released all his films through Fox.

What the critics said about
DANGEROUS YEARS

William A. Weaver
in *Motion Picture Herald:*

Some of the causes of juvenile delinquency, and some of the adult policies designed to offset them, are explored interestingly here in a melodrama forcefully directed by Arthur Pierson. . . . Some plot surprises are added for purposes of impact.

Marilyn is sixth from left

Ladies *of* the Chorus

A Columbia Picture (1948)

CAST

   *Adele Jergens, Marilyn Monroe, Rand Brooks, Nana Bryant, Eddie Garr,
Steven Geray, Bill Edwards, Marjorie Hoshelle, Frank Scannell,
Dave Barry, Alan Barry, Myron Healey, Robert Clarke, Gladys Blake,
Emmett Vogan.*

CREDITS

   *Produced by Harry A. Romm. Directed by Phil Karlson. Screen play
by Harry Sauber and Joseph Carol. From a story by Harry Sauber.
Photography by Frank Redman. Musical director, Mischa Bakaleinikoff.
Production numbers staged by Jack Boyle. Edited by Richard Fantl.*

SYNOPSIS

   May Martin (Adele Jergens), once a burlesque star, now dances in
the chorus, as does her daughter Peggy (Marilyn Monroe). When May
has an argument with Bubbles LaRue (Marjorie Hoshelle), a featured
dancer, Bubbles walks out on the show and Peggy takes her place.
Peggy becomes a success.

   When Peggy falls in love with wealthy young Randy Carroll (Rand
Brooks), May fears the outcome will be as heartbreaking as had been her
own marriage to a man of means and social position. She is convinced

With Rand Brooks

that Randy's mother (Nana Bryant) will disapprove of the match.

Unaware of Peggy's background, Randy's mother arranges an
engagement party for the two young people. At the gathering, the
bandleader recognizes Peggy and unwittingly reveals her identity. Peggy
is crushed, sure that her dream of marriage is over. But Randy's mother
comes through in an unexpected way. Convinced of the genuineness
of Peggy's love, she invents for the benefit of her surprised guests
a secret past in show business. Peggy is thus put at ease and murmurings
stilled before harm can be done. Nothing now stands in the way of
Peggy's and Randy's happiness. Reassured and free of responsibility
and concern for her daughter's future, May decides to marry her
beau of long standing, Billy Mackay (Eddie Garr), a comic with
the show.

Marilyn's performance in her second movie should have encouraged
some studio to put her under contract, but such was not the case.
Most of the studios already had a top glamour girl and probably feared
taking a chance with an unknown. She had been let go by Fox and this
was her only film for Columbia. Yet the potential for stardom was there.
Although still very young and immature as an actress, Marilyn even
then had a quality independent of her obvious good looks. She was
able to excite with a simple look or gesture. She sang two songs in this
film, "Every Baby Needs a Da Da Daddy" and "Anyone Can Tell I
Love You" by Allan Roberts and Lester Lee. The former number was
used in another Columbia film, "Okinawa," in 1952.

With Rand Brooks

What the critics said about
LADIES OF THE CHORUS

Tibor Krekes
in *Motion Picture Herald:*
   One of the bright spots is Miss Monroe's singing. She is pretty and, with her pleasing voice and style, she shows promise.

Marilyn fifth and Adele Jergens sixth from left

Love Happy

(Both pages) With Groucho Marx

A United Artists Release of a Mary Pickford Presentation (1950)

CAST

Harpo, Chico, and Groucho Marx, Ilona Massey, Vera-Ellen,
Marion Hutton, Paul Valentine, Eric Blore, Raymond Burr, Bruce Gordon,
Melville Cooper, Leon Belasco, Marilyn Monroe.

CREDITS

Produced by Lester Cowan. Directed by David Miller. Screen play by
Frank Tashlin and Mac Benoff. Based on a story by Harpo Marx.
Photography by William C. Mellor. Musical score by Ann Bonell.
Edited by Basil Wrangell and Al Joseph.

SYNOPSIS

Detective Sam Grunion (Groucho Marx) gives an account of
one of his cases, which concerns the missing Romanoff diamonds.
Madame Egilichi (Ilona Massey) and her gang, which consists of
the two Zoto brothers—Alphonse (Raymond Burr) and Hannibal

(Bruce Gordon)—and Throckmorton (Melville Cooper), have smuggled the diamonds into the United States in a sardine can with a special mark on it.

A group of actors trying to put together a musical show become involved in the case. They include Mike Johnson (Paul Valentine), who both manages the show and dances in it. He is in love with Maggie Phillips (Vera-Ellen), his leading dancer. Others in the show are Faustino the Great (Chico Marx) and singer Bunny Dolan (Marion Hutton). Rehearsing in an empty theater, the cast is sustained by Harpo (Harpo Marx), a mute, who steals food to keep them alive.

Naturally, he manages to steal the sardine can containing the diamonds. Madame Egilichi traces the can to the theater, and haunts the theater in an attempt to regain it. Ultimately, she is forced to become the show's backer.

On opening night the can is discovered. Harpo grabs it, and the gang pursues him to the roof, where a mad chase ensues in which Harpo dashes in and out of huge, flashing electric signs.

Grunion arrives at the theater on the trail of the diamonds. A gorgeous blonde (Marilyn Monroe) rushes up to him and begs his help because "men keep following me."

Grunion goes to the roof and meets Madame Egilichi with a gun in her hand. Harpo disappears forever with the sardine can.

The show is a success, and the narration ends as Grunion explains that Madame Egilichi became his wife.

Marilyn's third film appearance was just a walk-on. Her brief bit is a perfect example of the Marx Brothers' penchant for getting a laugh with a bizarre scene not directly related to the plot of the film.

Chico Marx and Marion Hutton

Harpo Marx and Ilona Massey

What the critics said about
LOVE HAPPY

T.M.P.
in the *New York Times:*

The Marx Brothers are loose again and have turned the Criterion's screen into a comic shambles. "Love Happy" is helter-skelter entertainment and one's estimation of the picture no doubt will be prejudiced according to one's fondness for the Marxes. Under the circumstances it is practically impossible to render an impartial verdict, or a satisfying one at that. But near as this spectator can balance the scales of judgment, "Love Happy" is a see-saw affair; sometimes the antics are incredibly funny, and pianissimo, please—sometimes the gags fall with a flat thud.

Joe Pihodna
in the *New York Herald Tribune:*

Thank goodness there's a little normality in a dizzy world. The Marx Brothers, in slightly amended form, are back in the cinema world and the event is an occasion for celebration. . . . Marx fans will get their money's worth. An aficionado asks only for certain time-tested maneuvers from the comedians. They will get them at the Criterion.

Archer Winston
in the *New York Post:*

The picture is both ingenious and lively, within the pattern previously set by the Marxes. Whether it will bring new joys to a generation that has not known them before, or recover hysterical merriment for oldsters who once split their sides over these antics are questions that experience alone can answer.

This department recognized more than it was able to greet with hearty guffaws, but that's only one person's uncertain response.

With Dan Dailey

With Barbara Smith, Joyce McKenzie, and Marion Marshall

A Ticket to Tomahawk

A Twentieth Century-Fox Picture (1950)

CAST

Dan Dailey, Anne Baxter, Rory Calhoun, Walter Brennan,
Charles Kemper, Connie Gilchrist, Arthur Hunnicutt, Will Wright,
Chief Yowlachie, Victor Sen Yung, Mauritz Hugo, Raymond Greenleaf,
Harry Carter, Harry Seymour, Robert Adler, Chief Thundercloud,
Marion Marshall, Joyce McKenzie, Marilyn Monroe, Barbara Smith.

CREDITS

Produced by Robert Bassler. Directed by Richard Sale. Screen
play by Mary Loos and Richard Sale. Photography by Harry Jackson.
Music by Cyril Mockridge. Edited by Harmon Jones. In Technicolor.

SYNOPSIS

Dawson (Mauritz Hugo), the owner of a stagecoach line, does not
want Engine One, the Emma Sweeney of the Tomahawk and Western
Railroad, to complete its run on time to Tomahawk, Colorado, in
1876. If the engine does not reach its destination on time, it will lose

its charter and will not be competition for his stage line. He hires a
gunman named Dakota (Rory Calhoun) to accomplish his ends. Engineer
Terence Sweeney (Walter Brennan) gets the engine to Epitaph, only
to learn that there are no rails from there to Dead Horse Point.

U.S. Marshal Dodge (Will Wright), wounded before he can aid the
engineer, deputizes his granddaughter Kit (Anne Baxter) to get the
engine to Tomahawk, promising to ride ahead when he recovers and
meet her there.

Kit determines to get the engine to the rails at Dead Horse Point
with the help of a mule team. She forces a drummer, Johnny Behind-the-
Deuces (Dan Dailey), to be the passenger needed to complete the run.

Dakota accompanies the group as does Madame Adelaide (Connie
Gilchrist), who is the boss of a troupe of showgirls (one of whom,
Clara, is played by Marilyn Monroe). The troupe intends to perform
in Tomahawk. During the journey Johnny does a song and dance
number with the girls.

Johnny persuades Indian leader Crooked Knife (Chief Thundercloud)
to help them get the engine to Dead Horse Point and not make war
upon them. He also makes Kit fall in love with him.

Dakota rides ahead to Dead Horse Point and fires shots into the
water tank there, unaware that the engine has an adequate supply of
water. The engine arrives safely and is placed on the rails ready to go.

Dakota is confronted with a bullet slug which proves he sabotaged the
water tank. While the engine is going at full speed, Dakota and
Johnny get into a fight. Dakota is knocked off and falls to the bottom
of a canyon. As Dawson and his men attack, Johnny sends up
smoke signals from the engine.

The signals are seen by Crooked Knife and his Indians and also by
Marshal Dodge, who had arrived in Tomahawk earlier. The Indians
and the marshal's posse rout the outlaws, and Pawnee (Chief Yowlachie),
Kit's bodyguard, kills Dawson.

The engine makes Tomahawk on time and the railroad company
is awarded its charter. Johnny embarks on a new career as a
railroad engineer and a new life with Kit.

Marilyn's role in this, her fourth film, was decorative, if minor. Her
most conspicuous contribution was the number she performed with
Dan Dailey and three girls called "Oh, What a Forward Young
Man You Are," written by Ken Darby and John Read.

Anne Baxter

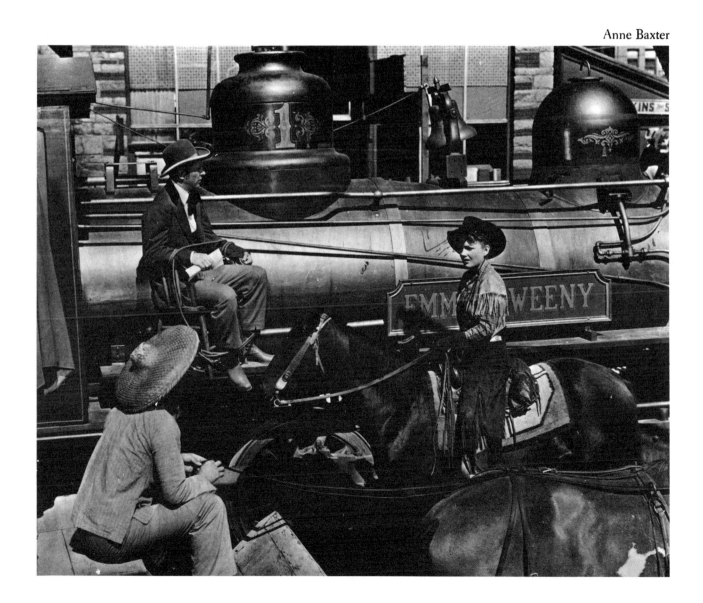

The Asphalt Jungle

A Metro-Goldwyn-Mayer Picture (1950)

CAST

Sterling Hayden, Louis Calhern, Jean Hagen, Sam Jaffe, James Whitmore, John McIntire, Marc Lawrence, Barry Kelley, Anthony Caruso, Teresa Celli, Marilyn Monroe, William Davis, Dorothy Tree, Brad Dexter, John Maxwell.

CREDITS

Produced by Arthur Hornblow, Jr. Directed by John Huston. Screen play by Ben Maddow and John Huston. From a novel by W. R. Burnett. Photography by Harold Rosson. Musical score by Miklos Rozsa. Edited by George Boemler.

SYNOPSIS

Doc Riedenschneider (Sam Jaffe), just out of prison, has planned a jewel store robbery. In on the robbery are Dix Handley (Sterling Hayden), Gus Minissi (James Whitmore), and Louis Ciavelli (Anthony Caruso). The job is financed by a bookie named Cobby (Marc Lawrence).

They plan to sell the stolen jewels to an influential lawyer, Alonzo D. Emmerich (Louis Calhern), who also acts as a fence. Nearly broke and knowing full well that he cannot pay for the jewels, he plans a double cross. He is able to put up a convincing front with the aid of his beautiful blonde mistress, Angela Phinlay (Marilyn Monroe), whom he introduces to everyone as his niece.

Handley joins in the robbery so that he can go home to Kentucky and buy back his family's farm. A girl named Doll Conovan (Jean Hagen) loves Handley, but he is afraid to show any feeling for her.

The robbery is accomplished, but the circuit to the burglar alarms in the district goes off. When Handley knocks a watchman's gun to the floor, it goes off and a bullet hits Ciavelli. They flee the scene. Doc and Handley take the jewels to Emmerich, who claims he doesn't have the money yet. A henchman of Emmerich's pulls a gun and demands the jewels. Handley shoots him, but is badly wounded himself. Doc takes Handley to Doll, who takes care of him.

The body of Emmerich's henchman is found. Cobby is the first to be arrested, and Emmerich a close second when Angela fails to back up

With Louis Calhern

Sam Jaffe, Sterling Hayden,
Anthony Caruso, James Whitmore

Sterling Hayden, Sam Jaffe,
Anthony Caruso

his alibi. Ciavelli dies from his bullet wound and Gus, who had called
a doctor for him, is arrested.

Doc is also caught, but Doll flees by car with Handley to Kentucky.
When Handley reaches his old home, he dies as a result of his wound.

Marilyn's fifth film was the one which called the public's attention to
her. Her seductive manner was tempered with a touch of naïveté that
intrigued audiences. The public began to wonder who she was.

Emmerich called Angela his niece in the film because the word
"mistress" in 1950 was still taboo in films. Such discretion is now out
of date, but the picture retains its position as one of Hollywood's all-time
greats, many critics still considering it among the best of its kind.

best one ever made. . . . This picture drives home the corollary thought that criminals are also human beings.

Among the happy results of this kind of treatment a set of absolutely wonderful performances may be listed. It would be unfair to single out a few for special praise.

Liza Wilson
in *Photoplay:*

This brutally frank story of crime and punishment in a Midwestern city was directed by two-time Academy Award winner, John Huston—son of the late Walter Huston. John's pictures are usually grim ("The Treasure of Sierra Madre"), but always dramatic and exciting. This time he exposes the behind-the-scenes details of the robbery of a jewelry store. . . . This picture is packed with stand-out performances. . . . There's a beautiful blonde, too, name of Marilyn Monroe, who plays Calhern's girl friend, and makes the most of her footage.

Bosley Crowther
in the *New York Times:*

Louis Calhern as the big lawyer who tries to pull a double cross and muffs it is exceptionally fluid and adroit and Sterling Hayden is sure-fire as a brazen hoodlum who just wants to go back home. Likewise Sam Jaffe does wonders as a coolheaded mastermind, James Whitmore is taut as a small "fixer" and John McIntire is crisp as a chief of police. But, then, everyone in the picture—which was produced incidentally, by M.G.M.—gives an unimpeachable performance. If only it all weren't so corrupt.

Howard Barnes
in the *New York Herald Tribune:*

It is a violent exhibition, dedicated to sluggings and large-scale jewel robberies, but Huston has made it a taut and engrossing melodrama. . . . Sterling Hayden is excellent in the part of the fast shooting Dix. . . . Incidentally, Jean Hagen is very good as the Doll who gets mixed up in a major robbery, James Whitmore gives a good account of himself as the sidekick of Dix and John McIntire, Marilyn Monroe and Anthony Caruso lend a documentary effect to a lurid exposition.

What the critics said about
THE ASPHALT JUNGLE

Archer Winsten
in the *New York Post:*

This picture has the authority of a blow in your solar plexus. It leaves you physically tired with sheer tension, participation and belief. It is the crime picture of this decade, and it may be the

(Facing page) With Anne Baxter, Bette Davis,
and George Sanders

All About Eve

A Twentieth Century-Fox Picture (1950)

CAST

Bette Davis, Anne Baxter, George Sanders, Celeste Holm, Gary Merrill, Hugh Marlowe, Thelma Ritter, Marilyn Monroe, Gregory Ratoff, Barbara Bates, Walter Hampden, Randy Stuart, Craig Hill.

CREDITS

Produced by Darryl F. Zanuck. Directed by Joseph L. Mankiewicz. Written for the screen by Joseph L. Mankiewicz. From the story "The Wisdom of Eve" by Mary Orr. Photography by Milton Krasner. Musical score by Alfred Newman. Edited by Barbara McLean.

SYNOPSIS

Eve Harrington (Anne Baxter), an ambitious aspiring actress, gets into the good graces of famous stage actress Margo Channing (Bette Davis) by telling Margo that she is a devoted fan. Convinced by her hard-luck story, Margo gives Eve a job as her secretary.

Eve takes in everybody except Margo's maid Birdie (Thelma Ritter). At a party Eve meets New York drama critic Addison DeWitt (George Sanders). Accompanying DeWitt is Miss Caswell (Marilyn Monroe), a curvy blonde whom DeWitt describes as his "protégé." Margo gets drunk and becomes angry with Eve, whom she is beginning to get wise to.

Eve gets the job of Margo's understudy in her play with the help of Margo's friend Karen (Celeste Holm). Margo arrives at the theater to read with Miss Caswell, who is up for a part in the play. She learns that Miss Caswell flopped but goes into a rage when she discovers that Eve has landed the understudy part.

Karen thinks that Margo is being unfair to Eve and they quarrel. Later, when Margo visits Karen at her country home, Karen makes sure that their car will be out of gas when they leave for the railroad station, where Margo is to catch a train to New York for her evening performance. Karen wants to give Eve her chance to go on.

Margo misses the train, and when Eve goes on in her place, Dewitt praises her performance. That night Eve had made a pass at the play's director, Bill Sampson (Gary Merrill), who is also Margo's boy-friend, but he had spurned her. DeWitt had witnessed the rejection.

Eve tries to get Karen to convince her husband, Lloyd (Hugh Marlowe), to give her the lead in a new play that he has written for Margo. She threatens to reveal that Karen had been responsible for her going

on in Margo's place. Karen is relieved when Margo decides not to do
the new play but to marry Bill.

At the New Haven tryout, Eve tells DeWitt that she plans to get
Lloyd to divorce Karen, marry her, and write plays for her. DeWitt angrily
rejoins that he knows many sordid facts about her past and insists that
she belongs to him. Eve tearfully gives up her plans involving Lloyd.

Eve receives the Sarah Siddons Award for her performance in Lloyd's
new play. At the presentation are all those who have befriended her
and whom she has used.

When Eve returns to her apartment that night she finds a girl named
Phoebe (Barbara Bates), who explains that she is a fan. Eve is flattered
by the girl's adulation. When DeWitt delivers the award statuette
which Eve had forgotten, Phoebe answers the door and takes it.

While Eve is in the other room, Phoebe poses with the statuette in
front of a mirror bowing to her image as if she had won the award.

"All About Eve" ranks as one of the most distinguished films
ever made. It was the recipient of many awards and rave reviews.

Marilyn had a small but showy role, as she had had in "The Asphalt
Jungle." She was remarkably convincing as a girl willing to sacrifice
anything to make the big time, though short on talent. Miss Caswell
was the foil to suggest DeWitt's lecherous qualities early in the story.
Marilyn's performance in her sixth film won her another Fox contract.

Barbara Bates

(Facing page)
Letf to right, Gregory Ratoff,
Anne Baxter, Gary Merrill,
Celeste Holm, George Sanders,
and Marilyn

Celeste Holm, Hugh Marlowe,
Bette Davis, and Anne Baxter

What the critics said about
ALL ABOUT EVE

Bosley Crowther
in the *New York Times:*

The good old legitimate theatre, the temple of
Thespis and Art, which has dished out a lot of high
derision of Hollywood in its time, had better be
able to take it as well as dish it out, because the
worm has finally turned with a venom and
Hollywood is dishing it back. In "All About Eve,"
a withering satire—witty, mature and worldly-
wise—which Twentieth Century-Fox and Joseph
L. Mankiewicz delivered to the Roxy yesterday,
the movies are letting Broadway have it with claws
out and no holds barred. If Thespis doesn't want
to take a beating, he'd better yell for George
Kaufman and Moss Hart.

As a matter of fact, Mr. Kaufman and Mr. Hart
might even find themselves outclassed by the
dazzling and devastating mockery that is brilliantly
packed into this film. For obviously, Mr.
Mankiewicz, who wrote and directed it, had been
sharpening his wits and his talents a long, long
time for just this go. Obviously, he had been
observing the theatre and its charming folks for
years with something less than an idolator's rosy
illusions and zeal. And now, with the excellent
assistance of Bette Davis and a truly sterling cast,
he is wading into the theatre's middle with all
claws slashing and settling a lot of scores.

Otis L. Guernsey, Jr.
in the *New York Herald Tribune:*

A brilliant writing-directing stint by Joseph L.
Mankiewicz has brightened up the autumn screen.
. . . As a director, he has spiced every foot of the
film with pointed or amusing detail, and he has
summoned a round of tiptop performances from
Bette Davis, Anne Baxter, George Sanders, Celeste
Holm and the others. The result is one of the
finest and most mature pictures to emerge from
Hollywood or anywhere else in years. . . . With its
slow emergence of evil through a mass of comedy,
"All About Eve" is an entertainment bonanza,
but it is at the same time a supremely adroit and
professional piece of cinema artistry.

Individual performances, all of the same high
quality, stand out only in size.

The Fireball

A Twentieth Century-Fox Release of a Thor Production (1950)

CAST

Mickey Rooney, Pat O'Brien, Beverly Tyler, Glenn Corbett, James Brown, Marilyn Monroe, Ralph Dumke, Bert Begley, Milburn Stone, Tom Flint, John Hedloe.

CREDITS

Produced by Bert Friedlob. Directed by Tay Garnett. Screen play by Tay Garnett and Horace McCoy. Photography by Lester White. Musical score by Victor Young. Edited by Frank Sullivan.

SYNOPSIS

Johnny Casar (Mickey Rooney) runs away from an orphanage run by Father O'Hara (Pat O'Brien) and gets a job in a beanery. He goes to a Rollerbowl where he meets Mary Reeves (Beverly Tyler), a champion roller skater who teaches him how to skate. He gets into races with Mack Miller (Glenn Corbett), a champion skater whom he dislikes intensely. At first he loses, but Mary shows him what he is doing wrong and he beats his rival.

Johnny gets a job with The Bears, roller skating speedway champions. Father O'Hara meets Johnny and tells him that he has always been aware of his whereabouts. The priest is proud and pleased that Johnny is making a name for himself. But as Johnny becomes a favorite with the crowds, success goes to his head and although he wins many games for his team he works by and for himself and not with the team.

Wildness is another ingredient of the new life. He becomes involved with many women—including Polly (Marilyn Monroe)—who are interested in him because he is a champion, not because they care about him for himself, as does Mary.

When Johnny contracts polio, Mary helps to nurse him back to health. He returns to work finally, but he still hasn't learned the meaning of team spirit. And then the big race arrives, the International. Instead of seeking personal glory, Johnny helps a young member of his team win the race for their team. Johnny has finally realized the truth about himself, and the unselfish act which demonstrates this inner change wins him the renewed respect of Father O'Hara and Mary's lasting love.

Marilyn's seventh film was an independent production released through Fox.

With James Brown and Mickey Rooney

What the critics said about
THE FIREBALL

H. H. T.
in the *New York Times:*

As a trimly budgeted, fairly picturesque handling of a new sports angle, "The Fireball" has a few good moments in the skating sequences, in Pat O'Brien's droll portrayal of the priest, and, paradoxically, during the early scenes of Mr. Rooney's vagrancy. In fact, here, when he is acting as normal as blueberry pie, Mr. Rooney's trouping is on a par with his excellent "Killer McCoy" three years ago.

James S. Barstow, Jr.
in the *New York Herald Tribune:*

In staging the screen play, written with Horace McCoy, Tay Garnett has taken considerable trouble in the early part of the new film at the Palace to make the character of "Fireball" Casar believable. The work is pulled apart in a contrived climax that gives no explanation for the conversion of a heel to a hero. . . Garnett has captured a lot of the color and excitement of roller-derby racing; that's about all there is to "The Fireball."

With Dick Powell

Right Cross

A Metro-Goldwyn-Mayer Picture (1950)

CAST

June Allyson, Dick Powell, Ricardo Montalban, Lionel Barrymore, Teresa Celli, Barry Kelley, Mimi Aguglia, Marianne Stewart, John Gallaudet, Wally Maher, Larry Keating, Ken Tobey, Bert Davidson, Marilyn Monroe.

CREDITS

Produced by Armand Deutsch. Directed by John Sturges. Screen play by Charles Schnee. Photography by Norbert Brodine. Music by David Raksin. Edited by James E. Newcom.

SYNOPSIS

Johnny Monterez (Ricardo Montalban), a champion prizefighter, has a chip on his shoulder because he is Mexican. His promoter, Sean O'Malley (Lionel Barrymore), who was once a top man in the fight game, now has only Johnny to rely on. Allan Goff (Barry Kelley), a top promoter, wants Johnny to fight for him, but Johnny has put him

Dick Powell and Ricardo Montalban

off. Johnny is in love with O'Malley's daughter, Pat (June Allyson), and for this reason does not want to sign with Goff.

One of Johnny's few friends is Rick Gavery (Dick Powell), a sports reporter. Rick is also in love with Pat, but realizes that she loves Johnny. To compensate for his loneliness, Rick takes to drink and women. (Marilyn Monroe has the bit part of a beautiful woman he is with in a nightclub.)

Johnny knows that his right hand is going bad and fears that his days as champion are numbered. He decides that he'd better sign with Goff and get some big money so that he can retire and take care of Pat and her father before his hand becomes useless to him.

Shortly after O'Malley learns that Johnny wants to leave him, the old promoter dies of a heart attack and Pat blames Johnny, unaware of the real reason for his decision. Johnny puts up his championship title for his last fight for the O'Malley organization in the hope that this move will draw in the crowds. However, Johnny loses the fight. He returns to his dressing room where Rick is waiting for him. Although he has not hurt his hand during the fight, during an argument with

Rick he throws the punch that breaks his hand.

Johnny returns to his training camp alone, but Rick and Pat follow him there. Rick convinces Johnny that he is still his friend; Pat persuades him that she now realizes he only wanted to help her. Johnny sees that she still loves him and is reconciled to the fact that he can no longer fight.

Although this was Marilyn's eighth film, she received no billing. We have entered her name at the end of the cast listing on our own.

Ricardo Montalban (second from right)

Dick Powell and Lionel Barrymore

(Right) Ricardo Montalban and June Allyson

What the critics said about
RIGHT CROSS

Archer Winsten
in the *New York Post:*

"Right Cross," at the Criterion, is a boxing story with a romance sidelighted by Mexican racial feeling. It doesn't come out of the grinder a great picture, but it does offer a few pleasures of its own. . . . "Right Cross" frankly functions on the entertainment level, but its incidental assumptions are worthy of encouragement because they bring the characters to life in terms of one current social problem.

Dorothy Masters
in the *New York Daily News:*

The movies are overdue with a picture like "Right Cross." It's long past time Hollywood took up the cudgels in defense of the plain old American majority, and it's good to have the shoe on the other foot for a change.

The significance of the Criterion's new film is not its sole recommendation, however. Outstanding dialogue, a wonderful sense of humor and a talented cast would make it exceptional film fare, with or without the lesson in sociology.

Frank Quinn
in the *New York Daily Mirror:*

The title will attract the males, who will recognize it as a fight picture. But it appeals also as a romantic story, neatly dovetailed into the fistic sequences.

John Sturges directed with neat balance between love-making and leather-pushing, for smooth continuity. The characters come alive. A thin thread of racial conflict seems superfluous. . . . "Right Cross" doesn't let down in action or heart appeal. It depicts some backstage skullduggery with realism. The fight sequences are thrilling and convincing

With Alan Hale, Jr.

Hometown Story

A Metro-Goldwyn-Mayer Picture (1951)

CAST

Jeffrey Lynn, Donald Crisp, Marjorie Reynolds, Alan Hale, Jr.,
Marilyn Monroe, Barbara Brown, Melinda Plowman, Kenny McEvoy,
Glenn Tryon, Byron Foulger, Griff Barnett, Virginia Campbell,
Harry Harvey, Nelson Leigh, Speck Noblitt.

CREDITS

Produced, directed and written by Arthur Pierson. Photography by
Lucien Andriot. Musical score by Louis Forbes. Edited by William Claxton.

SYNOPSIS

When Blake Washburn (Jeffrey Lynn) is defeated in his bid for
re-election to the state legislature, he returns to his home town and
takes over the editorship of the *Herald* newspaper upon his uncle's (Griff

Barnett) retirement. (Marilyn Monroe has the role of Miss Martin who works in the newspaper office.)

Blake blames big business forces for his defeat because the son of a wealthy manufacturer was the man who defeated him, and he uses the newspaper to go after the manufacturer, MacFarland (Donald Crisp), and others, claiming it is big business that is working against the best interests of the people.

Blake comes into conflict with his fiancée, Janice Hunt (Marjorie Reynolds), a schoolteacher, and Slim Haskins (Alan Hale, Jr.), a reporter on the *Herald* and Blake's friend, neither of whom agree with him. MacFarland comes to visit Blake and tries to convince him that everyone benefits from big business, but Blake refuses to change his point of view.

When Janice takes her class on a picnic, Katie (Melinda Plowman), Blake's kid sister, is trapped in a mine shaft after a landeslide. Blake and Slim join the rush to the scene. Although Katie is rescued by workmen, she has been hurt, as an examination by MacFarland's factory doctor discloses. MacFarland arranges for his plane to fly Katie to a hospital where a brain surgeon saves her life. After the operation she is placed in a respirator to recover. MacFarland tells Blake that the motor for the respirator was manufactured by his company.

Blake changes his attitude toward MacFarland and big business. Now there is room for a reconciliation with Janice as well as a change in his newspaper editorial policy.

Marilyn's ninth film was her third and last Metro-Goldwyn-Mayer picture.

What the critics said about
HOME TOWN STORY

With Jeffrey Lynn

Brog
in *Variety:*

Arthur Pierson wrote and directed, using a competent professional cast of such names as Jeffrey Lynn, Donald Crisp and Marjorie Reynolds in star spots. . . . Marilyn Monroe, Barbara Brown and Griff Barnett are up to script demands.

James D. Ivers
in *Motion Picture Herald:*

In short and simple terms, at times almost too simple, this hour-long offering attempts with no subtlety whatever a blanket defense of business. The story moves with some speed and there is an element of suspense at the end, even though it is too obviously constructed only to carry the message.

As Young

as You Feel

A Twentieth Century-Fox Picture (1951)

CAST

Monty Woolley, Thelma Ritter, David Wayne, Jean Peters, Constance Bennett, Marilyn Monroe, Allyn Joslyn, Albert Dekker, Clinton Sundberg, Minor Watson, Ludwig Stossel, Renie Riano, Wally Brown, Rusty Tamblyn, Roger Moore.

CREDITS

Produced by Lamar Trotti. Directed by Harmon Jones. Screen play by Lamar Trotti. Based on a story by Paddy Chayefsky. Photography by Joe MacDonald. Musical score by Cyril Mockridge. Edited by Robert Simpson.

SYNOPSIS

John Hodges (Monty Woolley) is forced to retire at sixty-five from his job at Acme Printing Services due to a policy of its parent company, Consolidated Motors. Hodges returns home and tells his son George (Allyn Joslyn), George's wife Della (Thelma Ritter), and their daughter Alice (Jean Peters), what happened. Only Alice gives him some genuine sympathy.

He goes to the company personnel office where Alice's fiancé, Joe Elliott (David Wayne), works. He complains to Joe and another employee, Erickson (Clinton Sundberg). Joe suggests that he write to the president of Consolidated Motors, but no one knows who he is. Hodges finds out that the president's name is Cleveland and formulates a plan.

Posing as Cleveland, with his hair and beard dyed black, Hodges sends a wire to the president of Acme, Louis McKinley (Albert Dekker), saying that he is arriving on an inspection tour. Not even the reassuring presence of his beautiful secretary, Harriet (Marilyn Monroe), can calm McKinley's nervousness.

The imposter arrives and Joe recognizes him, but Erickson is fooled. McKinley arranges a dinner for Hodges at which the supposed president is to make a speech. McKinley introduces him to his wife, Lucille (Constance Bennett), who becomes infatuated with him.

Hodges arranges that all retired personnel should be rehired if they

With Albert Dekker

wish to return and then returns home with his deception at an end,
feeling confident that his job is now secure.

However, there is an unanticipated turn of events. His speech causes
the company's stock to go up. And when it is discovered that he was the
imposter, the real Cleveland (Minor Watson) comes to see him, as
does Lucille, who has left McKinley, thinking he no longer loves her.

Joe is promoted in the personnel department when Erickson tries to tell
on Hodges. McKinley comes to get Lucille at the Hodges' home. He fires
Hodges and takes his wife away, barking epithets at the interfering
Cleveland. When his wife informs him that he has just been shouting
at the president of the parent company, McKinley faints.

Cleveland offers Hodges an important job with the company; but when
Hodges expresses his preference for his old job, Cleveland assures him
that McKinley will not be allowed to interfere with his return. Everything
ends well, with Hodges proving that age has nothing to do with
intelligence or ability.

Marilyn's tenth film and her first under her new Fox contract found
her stock going up. Continuing to cast her in parts which called
for a sexy blonde, Fox was seeing to it that her scenes were more numerous.

What the critics said about
AS YOUNG AS YOU FEEL

Bosley Crowther
in the *New York Times*:

This unpretentious little picture, which Lamar Trotti has written and produced and which Harmon Jones has directed in a deliciously nimble comic style, is a vastly superior entertainment so far as ingenuity and taste are concerned, and it certainly confronts its audience on a much more appropriately adult plane. . . . Albert Dekker is mighty amusing as a fatheaded small-business boss, Marilyn Monroe is superb as his secretary. . . .

Frank Quinn
in the *New York Daily Mirror*:

Cast and story set amusing situations, but neither explosive nor frequent enough. . . . Curvy Marilyn Monroe is a secretary.

Archer Winsten
in the *New York Post*:

It is an uncommonly pleasing picture if no critical solvents are applied to it. Being short on probability and long on popular laugh devices of plot and character, it can be recommended highly to most of the people most of the time.

With Wally Brown, Monty Woolley, and Albert Dekker

Love Nest

A Twentieth Century-Fox Picture (1951)

CAST

June Haver, William Lundigan, Frank Fay, Marilyn Monroe, Jack Paar, Leatrice Joy, Henry Kulky, Marie Blake, Patricia Miller, Maude Wallace, Joe Ploski, Martha Wentworth, Faire Binney, Caryl Lincoln, Robert H. Young, Michael Ross.

CREDITS

Produced by Jules Buck. Directed by Joseph Newman. Screen play by I. A. L. Diamond. Based on a novel by Scott Corbett. Photography by Lloyd Ahern. Musical score by Cyril Mockridge. Edited by J. Watson Webb, Jr.

SYNOPSIS

Jim Scott (William Lundigan) returns from army duty overseas and with his wife, Connie (June Haver) moves into an old building she has bought in New York. Although they get an income from renting out rooms in it, the building causes problems for Jim and keeps him from writing a novel.

Roberta Stevens (Marilyn Monroe), an ex-WAC and Jim's friend from army days, comes to live in the building, much to the discomfort of Connie. On the other hand, Jim's pal Ed Forbes (Jack Paar) is quite happy that Roberta is living there.

Charley Patterson (Frank Fay) becomes a tenant and marries another tenant, Eadie Gaynor (Leatrice Joy). He loans money to Jim to keep him from losing the building, but Jim and Connie have suspicions about his means of making an income. Finally the truth comes out. Charley is exposed as a Casanova who has taken money from rich widows. But when Charley is arrested, Eadie stands by him. Charley explains that the widows had been just as anxious to get money that they thought he had as he had been to get theirs.

Charley advises the police that he gave Jim money to keep him from telling about him. Thereupon Jim is arrested and berates Charley in jail for his lies. But Charley explains that he had to get Jim into jail so that he could dictate his memoirs to him. He urges Jim to keep half the

With Jack Paar

With June Haver

money he receives for them and to give the other half to Eadie. Jim
is released and gets the memoirs published.

With the help of the money from this, Jim and Connie are able to
renovate the building and Eadie is freed of money problems. Charley is
sentenced to prison for a year and a half. Upon his release he is reunited
with Eadie to become the father of twins.

Marilyn's eleventh film saw her getting bigger billing. The public was
now becoming quite aware of her presence in a film. Appearing opposite
Marilyn in the part of a wolfish lawyer was Jack Paar. Paar had appeared
previously in minor roles at RKO, but it was in the television medium
that he was to prove himself.

Brog
in *Variety:*

There are only a few fresh lines and situations in the script, and they are not enough to add any punch to a rather "dated" theme, no matter how hard the cast toppers try to keep the laughs going. . . . Marilyn Monroe is tossed in to cause jealousy between the landlords. . . . The Jules Buck production supervision is adequate for physical polish, but short on story and script guidance.

M. Q., Jr.
in *Motion Picture Herald:*

This is a mildly amusing comedy revolving around the problems of June Haver and William Lundigan, a young couple, in their efforts to make a financial success of their investment in a small New York apartment house and at the same time stay happily married. . . . The story by I. A. L. Diamond from the novel by Scott Corbett is crowded with incidents, some of which are funny. The direction by Joseph Newman brings out quiet humor and keeps away from slapstick.

Film Daily:

Lightly skipping about in its treatment of a G.I.'s postwar investment, engineered by his wife while he was overseas, in a rundown house in the Gramercy Park section of Manhattan, "Love Nest" is a mild variety of comedy which gets a considerable boost from the expert talents—in that line—of Frank Fay. Rarely seen, he registers here as a smoothie, glib and ultra sophisticated, handy with the correct word on the correct occasion. Leatrice Joy is also present in this number. She gives mature warmth to the proceedings. Marilyn Monroe has that other quality, while William Lundigan, an author, and June Haver play at being married and troubled with their creaky domicile.

With Frank Fay and Jack Paar

With Zachary Scott

Let's Make It Legal

A Twentieth Century-Fox Picture (1951)

CAST

Claudette Colbert, Macdonald Carey, Zachary Scott, Barbara Bates, Robert Wagner, Marilyn Monroe, Frank Cady, Jim Hayward, Carol Savage, Paul Gerrits, Betty Jane Bowen, Vici Raaf, Ralph Sanford, Harry Denny, Harry Harvey, Sr.

CREDITS

Produced by Robert Bassler. Directed by Richard Sale. Screen play by F. Hugh Herbert and I. A. L. Diamond. Story by Mortimer Braus. Photography by Lucien Ballard. Musical score by Cyril Mockridge. Edited by Robert Fritch.

SYNOPSIS

Miriam Halsworth (Claudette Colbert) divorces her husband of twenty years, Hugh (Macdonald Carey), publicity director for a fashionable hotel. One of the reasons for the divorce is Hugh's love for gambling.

Miriam begins to get on the nerves of her son-in-law, Jerry Denham (Robert Wagner), having come to live with him and her daughter Barbara (Barbara Bates).

Victor Macfarland (Zachary Scott), a wealthy industrialist who once courted Miriam, comes to stay at the hotel. She had married Hugh after Victor left town without any explanation. When Victor finds out that she is divorced he begins to take an interest in her again.

Hugh is still in love with Miriam but he will not admit it. He begins seeing Joyce (Marilyn Monroe), a beautiful blonde at the hotel, hoping to make Miriam jealous. Joyce, for her part, has her eyes on Macfarland's money.

Victor and Miriam decide to marry, but he has to return to Washington on business first. Before he goes, he reveals that he and Hugh had rolled dice to see who would marry her twenty years ago, and that when he lost, he left town.

With Macdonald Carey,
Zachary Scott, and Claudette Colbert

Miriam becomes furious and informs Hugh that she is going to destroy
his prize rosebushes which she still has. When Hugh tries to sneak them
away at night, he is arrested. The story hits the papers and Miriam is
mentioned as being engaged to Victor. Enraged, Victor telephones her
and complains vehemently about his name being involved in the case.

Miriam tells Victor off and hangs up. Hugh shows her the dice he used
to win her from Victor. She sees that they are loaded and realizes that
Hugh had cheated so that he wouldn't lose her. Convinced that Hugh
still loves her, Miriam reconciles with him.

Marilyn continued the pattern established by her previous films in her
twelfth celluloid venture. Again she is the "beautiful blonde" who trades
on her looks to get what she wants.

What the critics said about
LET'S MAKE IT LEGAL

Frank Quinn
in the *New York Daily Mirror:*

Claudette Colbert is a capable farceur, but she cannot make "Let's Make It Legal" as merry as it was hoped. While she is on the Roxy screen the comedy skips along, but when her co-stars take over the plot labors.

It suffers from a weak script and incredible characterizations by Macdonald Carey and Zachary Scott. . . . Marilyn Monroe parades her shapely chassis for incidental excitement.

"Let's Make It Legal" is a valiant effort by Claudette Colbert, who cannot overcome the handicaps.

Wanda Hale
in the *New York Daily News:*

The Roxy's "Let's Make It Legal" is an inconsistent farce that luckily has sufficient saving graces, the predominating benefit being performances by the popular and comedy-wise co-stars, Claudette Colbert and Macdonald Carey. Their presences and a satisfactory amount of bright dialogue counteract strained farcical situations and the indifferent story. . . . Marilyn Monroe is amusing in a brief role as a beautiful shapely blonde who has her eye on Zachary Scott and his millions.

Clash by Night

An RKO Radio Release of a Jerry Wald-Norman Krasna Production (1952)

CAST
  Barbara Stanwyck, Paul Douglas, Robert Ryan, Marilyn Monroe,
J. Carrol Naish, Keith Andes, Silvio Minciotti.

CREDITS
  *Produced by Harriet Parsons. Directed by Fritz Lang. Screen play by
Alfred Hayes. Based on the play by Clifford Odets. Photography by
Nicholas Musuraca. Musical score by Roy Webb. Edited by George J. Amy.*

SYNOPSIS
  Mae Doyle (Barbara Stanwyck) returns to her home town after many
years, a tired and cynical woman. Her brother Joe (Keith Andes) is not
too pleased that she is back. He is in love with Peggy (Marilyn Monroe),
a fish cannery worker, and has fears that she may turn out to be like
his sister.
  Mae meets Jerry (Paul Douglas), a fishing boat skipper, and is attracted
by his qualities of gentleness and simplicity. Married to Jerry, she finds
contentment in motherhood, but ultimately becomes restless.
  She finds herself drawn to Jerry's friend Earl (Robert Ryan), a

With Robert Ryan

projectionist in a movie theater, even though she knows he is not good
for her. An affair develops and she decides to leave Jerry. Meanwhile,
Jerry's uncle, Vince (J. Carrol Naish), has hinted to Jerry about Mae
and Earl, but Jerry refuses to believe it.

Finally Mae admits the truth to Jerry, who immediately seeks out Earl
and nearly kills him in a fight. Mae learns that Jerry has taken their
baby to his boat. When Earl tries to persuade her to leave with him
without the baby, she realizes that he really doesn't care about anything
but himself and that her attraction to him was not love at all.

Mae returns to Jerry whom she has loved all along without realizing it
and begs him to forgive her for all the unhappiness she has caused him,
promising to be a good wife and mother from now on. Jerry relents
and takes her back.

Marilyn's thirteenth film found her playing her most important role to
date. Fox loaned her to RKO for the part and she made the most of her
chance. Working with such professionals as Barbara Stanwyck, Paul
Douglas and Robert Ryan, Marilyn held her own. The public loved her;
even the revelation that she had posed for that famous calendar did not
hurt her career, which, of course, it shouldn't have. Critics were also
taken with Marilyn and devoted more space to her performance in their
reviews of this film.

With Keith Andes

What the critics said about
CLASH BY NIGHT

Kate Cameron
in the *New York Daily News:*

"Clash By Night," which Harriet Parsons produced for the Wald-Krasna unit at RKO, is a tense, dramatic film based on a domestic problem. . . . Marilyn Monroe, who is the new blonde bombshell of Hollywood, manages to look alluring in blue jeans. She plays the secondary role of the cannery worker, Peggy, with complete assurance, and she and young Andes make their marks on the screen against the stiff competition given them by the three principals.

Irene Thirer
in the *New York Post:*

That gorgeous example of bathing beauty art (in denim), Marilyn Monroe, cast as Miss Stanwyck's gay, excitement-craving future sister-in-law, is a real acting threat to the season's screen blondes.

Alton Cook
in the *New York World Telegram and Sun:*

Barbara Stanwyck is off on another of her expert emotional rampages in "Clash By Night" at the Paramount. This Clifford Odets play gives her much more than her usual substance in the way of story and character.

Before going on any further with a report on "Clash By Night," perhaps we should mention the first full-length glimpse the picture gives us of Marilyn Monroe as an actress. The verdict is gratifyingly good.

This girl has a refreshing exuberance, an abundance of girlish high spirits. She is a forceful actress, too, when crisis comes along. She has definitely stamped herself as a gifted new star, worthy of all that fantastic press agentry. Her role here is not very big but she makes it dominant.

With Robert Ryan and Keith Andes

With Keith Andes

We're Not *Married*

A Twentieth Century-Fox Picture (1952)

CAST

Ginger Rogers, Fred Allen, Victor Moore, Marilyn Monroe, David Wayne, Eve Arden, Paul Douglas, Eddie Bracken, Mitzi Gaynor, Louis Calhern, Zsa Zsa Gabor, James Gleason, Paul Stewart, Jane Darwell, Alan Bridge, Harry Goler, Victor Sutherland, Tom Powers, Maurice Cass, Maude Wallace, Margie Liszt, Richard Buckley, Ralph Dumke, Lee Marvin, Marjorie Weaver, O. Z. Whitehead, Harry Harvey, Selmer Jackson.

CREDITS

Produced by Nunnally Johnson. Directed by Edmund Goulding. Screen play by Nunnally Johnson. Adapted by Dwight Taylor. From a story by Gina Kaus and Jay Dratler. Photography by Leo Tover. Musical score by Cyril Mockbridge. Edited by Louis Loeffler.

SYNOPSIS

Melvin Bush (Victor Moore), a Justice of the Peace, performs marriage ceremonies a few days before his license is actually valid. He is unaware of this mistake until two and a half years later, at which time letters are sent to the various couples. Five couples thus suddenly get the news that they are not, and never have been, really married.

In Mississippi, Annabel Norris (Marilyn Monroe) has won the title of Mrs. Mississippi and is now eligible for the Mrs. America contest. Her husband, Jeff (David Wayne), objects to the manner in which her "career" is interfering with her duties as housewife and mother of their baby. When they get the letter telling them that they are not legally married, Jeff is as gleeful as Annabel's manager, Duffy (James Gleason), is perturbed. However, Annabel realizes that she can now enter the Miss Mississippi contest. Jeff admits defeat and he and the baby later watch as Annabel wins the title of Miss Mississippi. The episode ends with their second wedding.

The other four couples receiving letters are played by Ginger Rogers and Fred Allen, Paul Douglas and Eve Arden, Eddie Bracken and Mitzi Gaynor, Louis Calhern and Zsa Zsa Gabor.

Marilyn's fourteenth picture found her performing again with a stellar cast. She later did a similar type of film for Fox, "O. Henry's Full House."

With David Wayne

With James Gleason

With David Wayne

What the critics said about
WE'RE NOT MARRIED

Otis L. Guernsey, Jr.
in the *New York Herald Tribune:*

Nunnally Johnson has a picnic with marriage in "We're Not Married" at the Roxy, and his good time is shared by all. . . . With David Wayne and Marilyn Monroe (who looks as though she had been carved out of cake by Michelangelo), it becomes a reason for a kitchen-bound husband to demand that his wife drop her busy activities as a beauty contest winner and return to the home.

Archer Winsten
in the *New York Post:*

Chalk up a direct hit for producer-writer Nunnally Johnson, director Edmund Goulding and their all-star cast in "We're Not Married" at the Roxy. This happy compilation of five episodes . . . studies marriage with admirable changes of pace and content. The range is from sharp satire to touching sentiment, from crass commercialism to deadly boredom. There isn't a dud in the lot of them, and there are many moments of delicious observation. . . . All performances . . . are at the top of their individual forms.

Alton Cook
in the *New York World-Telegram and Sun:*

Nunnally Johnson has found a spring of bubbling humor and turned it into a picture full of delightful effervescence. . . . Marilyn Monroe supplies the beauty at which she is Hollywood's currently foremost expert, and David Wayne adds his wry relish for humor.

Kate Cameron
in the *New York Daily News:*

One big reason for cheering over the Roxy Theatre's latest comedy film, "We're Not Married," is that it has brought Fred Allen back to the screen. Allen doesn't take over the picture, but in the episode wherein he and Ginger Rogers co-star he is in top comedy form. . . . Ginger demonstrates again that she is a clever comedienne, as she and Allen go through their routines as a husband-and-wife radio team that builds up great popularity and prosperity from their breakfast chatter. . . . The other episodes, all but one of which are of humorous content, are well played by their principals. Marilyn Monroe and David Wayne perform their roles well, the former representing a

With David Wayne (holding baby)

successful entrant in the "Mrs. America" beauty contest, the latter as her disgruntled husband.

Eve Arden and Paul Douglas are funny as a bored couple. . . . Louis Calhern is smooth in the role of a rich husband whose young wife plots to make a good thing of the community property laws of her state. Zsa Zsa Gabor has little to do as the scheming wife but look attractive, and that she does to perfection.

Eddie Bracken and Mitzi Gaynor are the principals in the only episode that borders on the pathetic. The incident which involves them in a matrimonial tangle might easily have turned tragic, but fate and Nunnally Johnson, who produced the picture and wrote the screen play, decreed otherwise.

Don't Bother to Knock

With Richard Widmark

With Donna Corcoran and Jim Backus

A Twentieth Century-Fox Picture (1952)

CAST

Richard Widmark, Marilyn Monroe, Anne Bancroft, Donna Corcoran, Jeanne Cagney, Lurene Tuttle, Elisha Cook, Jr., Jim Backus, Verna Felton, Willis B. Bouchey, Don Beddoe, Gloria Blondell, Grace Hayle, Michael Ross.

CREDITS

Produced by Julian Blaustein. Directed by Roy Baker. Screen play by Daniel Taradash. Based on a novel by Charlotte Armstrong. Photography by Lucien Ballard. Musical direction by Lionel Newman. Edited by George A. Gittens.

SYNOPSIS

Jed Towers (Richard Widmark), an airline pilot, stays at a New York hotel where his girl, Lyn Leslie (Anne Bancroft), is a singer.

When Lyn tells Jed that she no longer wants to see him because he is too hard-boiled a character, he returns to his room to sulk. His musings are interrupted by the appearance of a girl in the window of the room opposite his. Since he is on the outs with his own girl, he decides to investigate the possibilities here. It turns out that the girl is named Nell (Marilyn Monroe) and she is glad to have the boredom of an evening's

With Elisha Cook, Jr.

baby sitting broken up by the friendly stranger. Soon the pair become more than friendly.

When a kiss is interrupted by the sudden appearance of the little girl, Bunny (Donna Corcoran), Nell flies into a rage and sends the child back to her room crying. It seems that Nell has become convinced that Jed is her fiancé who had been lost in a plane during the war. Jed's sympathy is aroused when he realizes that Nell is mentally unbalanced.

The next interruption is a knock at the door, and Nell makes Jed hide in the bathroom. It is Eddie (Elisha Cook, Jr.), Nell's uncle, an elevator operator who got the baby-sitting job for her in the first place. He makes the mistake of saying something about Nell's fiancé which upsets her so much that she strikes him with an ash tray. Alarmed, Jed returns, reassured to find Eddie not seriously hurt. A woman appears at the door demanding an explanation for all the commotion. By now Jed is eager to get away, but he must first make sure that Bunny will be all right. After seeing that she is on the bed and extracting a promise from Eddie to look after things, he leaves the scene.

He meets Lyn and tells her about Nell. Lyn is amazed at the sympathy he displays for the girl. Suddenly Jed realizes that Bunny had not been in her own bed in the room when he looked, and he rushes back. Meanwhile, Nell has come to feel that Bunny was responsible for Jed's leaving and has decided to make the child pay. When Jed re-enters the room he finds Bunny tied up and Bunny's mother (Lurene Tuttle) battling with Nell. He separates them, and Nell flees.

A search ensues until Nell is discovered near the lobby with a razor in her hand, on the verge of suicide. Jed comes upon the scene to find a crowd gathered around her and Lyn taking the lead in an attempt to dissuade her. When he asks Nell for the razor, she hands it over meekly. He is able to convince her also that he is not her fiancé, and she comes to the realization that her fiancé is, in fact, dead. Policemen arrive and she leaves with them willingly, assured by Jed that they will take her to a hospital where she will be helped.

After Nell has been taken away, Lyn reconciles with Jed, now persuaded that he is, after all, a compassionate man—not the unfeeling person she had judged him to be.

Marilyn's fifteenth film found her in her first dramatic starring role. It was a difficult part for her. Up to that time, she had played a series of sexy blondes, and for her suddenly to be cast as a psychotic character came as a surprise. She played the role as she saw it and, although there was a difference of opinion among the critics as to the quality of her performance, the prevailing judgment was favorable. Marilyn apparently chose to portray Nell in terms of arrested emotional development, which seems in keeping with the intent of the script's author.

With Anne Bancroft and Richard Widmark

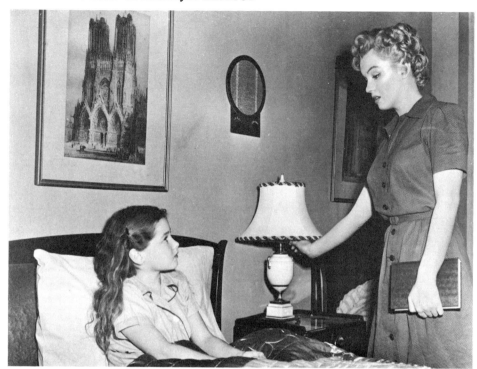

With Donna Corcoran

What the critics said about
DON'T BOTHER TO KNOCK

Archer Winsten
in the *New York Post:*

In "Don't Bother to Knock," at the Globe, they've thrown Marilyn Monroe into the deep dramatic waters, sink or swim, and while she doesn't really do either, you might say that she floats. With that figure what else can she do, and what would be better?

At first Miss Monroe gives a somewhat mannered impression of not being quite all there. Her dreamy monotone as she goes through the preliminaries of accepting a baby-sitting job with strangers in a Manhattan hotel may be considered a limitation of her acting ability. But as it turns out, this is not so at all. She really is slightly insane. . . . Sticklers for the niceties of psychotic behavior may pick at this or that in Miss Monroe's concept, but I thought she was surprisingly good, considering her lack of dramatic seasoning and her abundance of showgirl attributes. I could be prejudiced, though.

Otis L. Guernsey, Jr.
in the *New York Herald Tribune:*

Miss Monroe's part is that of a baby sitter who has all the right measurements but not all her marbles. . . . Miss Monroe is hushed and silky throughout these events, muffling the edge of hysteria in a childlike wistfulness.

Bosley Crowther
in the *New York Times:*

It requires a good deal to play a person who is strangely jangled in the head. And, unfortunately, all the equipment that Miss Monroe has to handle the job are a childishly blank expression and a provokingly feeble, hollow voice. With these she makes a game endeavor to pull something out of the role, but it looks as though she and her director, Roy Baker, were not quite certain what.

Frank Quinn
in the *New York Daily Mirror:*

Marilyn Monroe, whose screen roles have had little import except to show her natural physical attributes, now emerges in "Don't Bother to Knock" at the Globe as more than a sexy dame. She has good dramatic promise.

Richard Widmark shares star billing in the Twentieth Century-Fox melodrama but fizzles in the light of the new beauty. She is a provocative woman even in the drab costume of a poor hireling. She is what the movies need, a few more like her and the industry would thrive. . . . Miss Monroe's delineation of the deranged beauty is a surprise. She is completely in charge of the role, the direction of which merits praise for young Britisher Roy Baker. . . . "Don't Bother to Knock" has good pace, intriguing story and many assets—of which Marilyn Monroe is the most important.

With Cary Grant

Monkey Business

A Twentieth Century-Fox Picture (1952)

CAST

Cary Grant, Ginger Rogers, Charles Coburn, Marilyn Monroe, Hugh
Marlowe, Henri Letondal, Robert Cornthwaite, Larry Keating, Douglas
Spencer, Esther Dale, George Winslow, Emmett Lynn.

CREDITS

Produced by Sol C. Siegel. Directed by Howard Hawks. Screen play by
Ben Hecht, Charles Lederer and I. A. L. Diamond. Story by Harry Segall.
Photography by Milton Krasner. Musical score by Leigh Harline. Edited
by William B. Murphy.

SYNOPSIS

Dr. Barnaby Fulton (Cary Grant), a research chemist, has been
experimenting to find a formula to restore youthful vigor.

One day one of the chimpanzees used for experiments gets out of his

With Cary Grant and Ginger Rogers

(Both pictures)
With Cary Grant

cage. He mixes various chemicals and pours the compound into the open
cradle of a water cooler in the lab. The mixture mingles with water when
the janitor puts a fresh bottle onto the cooler. Fulton drinks some of his
latest formula to test its effects and takes some water from the cooler to
wash it down. He begins to feel peppy, completely unaware that it is the
mixture that the chimp made which has restored him to youthful vigor
and not his own.

When Fulton leaves, acting like a college boy, his boss, Oxley (Charles
Coburn), sends his secretary, Lois Laurel (Marilyn Monroe), to find
him. When she does, he takes her swimming, roller skating, and riding at
fast speed in a new car. The formula wears off, and his wife Edwina
(Ginger Rogers) overlooks the extremes of his behavior.

Later at Fulton's lab, Edwina takes some of Fulton's formula and also
some water from the cooler. She begins to act like an adolescent and almost
causes a scandal when she makes her husband take her to a hotel for a
second honeymoon. When the formula wears off, Edwina, too, comes
back to normal.

However, Fulton and Edwina use water from the cooler to make coffee,
unaware that it had been the water in the first place that contained the

With Cary Grant and Charles Coburn

youth restorative. This time they revert together, but to a still earlier stage.
Behaving like unruly children, they make a shambles out of a board of
directors meeting and go home. Then Fulton gets some neighborhood
children to tie an old flame of Edwina's, Harvey Entwhistle (Hugh
Marlowe), to a tree while he crops off Harvey's hair.

Meanwhile, Edwina has fallen asleep on the bed in her home. While she
is asleep, a neighbor's baby crawls into the room. She awakes, back to
normal once more, but when she sees the baby, she fears the worst.
Convinced it is actually her husband, she rushes to Oxley in a panic. But
Fulton has returned to the lab where he has fallen asleep. When he wakes
up, he is back to normal again.

Oxley and his board of directors also have taken some water from the
cooler with disastrous results. They all revert to a juvenile level of
behavior, with Oxley even chasing Miss Laurel and squirting seltzer water
at her. They, too, return to normal ultimately.

Fulton and Edwina are relieved that he did not perfect the formula,
after all, having experienced the hazards of a temporary return to youth.
Fulton laughs at the thought of seeing Oxley trying to get the chimp to mix
another batch of formula.

What the critics said about
MONKEY BUSINESS

Archer Winsten
in the *New York Post:*

Marilyn Monroe, described by Grant as "half child" and counter-described by Rogers with "not the visible half," poses and walks in a manner that must be called suggestive. What she suggests is something that this picture seems to have on its mind much of the time, with or without the rejuvenation.

Paul V. Beckley
in the *New York Herald Tribune:*

Not having seen Miss Monroe before, I know now what that's all about, and I've no dissenting opinions to offer. She disproves more than adequately the efficacy of the old stage rule about not turning one's back to the audience.

With Ginger Rogers and Cary Grant

With Cary Grant and Charles Coburn

Bosley Crowther
in the *New York Times*:

Mr. Grant and Miss Rogers as the couple who partake of the concoction that makes them young—or, at least, makes them behave like children, which is something else again; Charles Coburn as a drug manufacturer, Marilyn Monroe as his secretary and many more throw themselves into the nonsense with a fine and abandoned will.

Janet Graves
in *Photoplay*:

Marilyn Monroe garners laughs and whistles, bouncing in and out as a secretary who can't type. Typing skill, however, is the only attribute which the lady appears to be lacking in.

Kate Cameron
in the *New York Daily News*:

Cary Grant and Ginger Rogers have let down their hair in "Monkey Business," the 20th Century-Fox comedy now occupying the Roxy Theatre screen. The stars and their colleagues in the film put on a series of monkey-shines that would put a chimpanzee to shame. The audience loves the goings-on, attesting to their enjoyment by hearty laughter. . . . Ginger and Cary are assisted in this amusing nonsense by Marilyn Monroe, who can look and act dumber than any of the screen's current blondes.

O. Henry's Full House

Marilyn is accosted by Charles Laughton

A Twentieth Century-Fox Picture (1952)
Based on five stories by O. Henry

"The Cop and the Anthem"

CAST

Charles Laughton, Marilyn Monroe, David Wayne, Thomas Browne Henry, Richard Karlan, Erno Verebes, Nico Lek, William Vedder, Billy Wayne.

CREDITS

Produced by Andre Hakim. Directed by Henry Koster. Screen play by Lamar Trotti. Photography by Lloyd Ahern. Musical Score by Alfred Newman. Edited by Nick De Maggio.

SYNOPSIS

Soapy (Charles Laughton) is a bum but a most elegant and gentlemanly one. He confides to Horace (David Wayne), a fellow bum, that he plans to have himself arrested for committing a minor crime and thus enable himself to spend the oncoming winter months in a nice warm jail. However, all attempts fail. He even tries to accost a woman (Marilyn Monroe) on the streets in the hope that she will scream for police, but when he realizes that she is actually a streetwalker, he is the one who flees.

When Soapy and his pal hear music coming from a church they decide to go in and warm themselves. Once inside, Soapy begins to have some second thoughts about his life, and he makes up his mind to get a job and

(Above) Farley Granger and Jeanne Crain
in "The Gift of the Magi"

Facing page:
(Top left) Dale Robertson
and Richard Widmark in "The Clarion Call"
(Top, right) Anne Baxter in "The Last Leaf"
(Bottom) Kathleen Freeman, Fred Allen,
Oscar Levant, and Lee Asker in
"The Ransom of Red Chief"

reform. So preoccupied is he with his vision of the new life that he doesn't
see a policeman who has spotted the pair. His pal escapes, but Soapy is
arrested for vagrancy and sentenced to ninety days by the judge, thus
putting an end to his plans for reform.

This entire film was produced by Andre Hakim and scored by Alfred
Newman. The names of the other stories and their main players and
credits are as follows:

"The Clarion Call"—Dale Robertson, Richard Widmark. Directed by
Henry Hathaway. Screen play by Richard Breen. Photography by
Lucien Ballard. Edited by Nick De Maggio.

"The Last Leaf"—Anne Baxter, Jean Peters, Gregory Ratoff. Directed by
Jean Negulesco. Screen play by Ivan Goff and Ben Roberts. Photography
by Joe MacDonald. Edited by Nick De Maggio.

"The Ransom of Red Chief"—Fred Allen, Oscar Levant, Lee Aaker.
Directed by Howard Hawks. Screen play by Nunnally Johnson.
Photography by Milton Krasner. Edited by William B. Murphy.

"The Gift of the Magi"—Jeanne Crain, Farley Granger. Directed by
Henry King. Screen play by Walter Bullock. Photography by Joe
MacDonald. Edited by Barbara McLean.

Unlike "We're Not Married," which had five stories within a story, the
episodes in Marilyn's seventeenth film were entirely unrelated to each other.

What the critics said about
O. HENRY'S FULL HOUSE

Bosley Crowther
in the *New York Times:*

   True to the style of the author, who was right in
the popular groove, it is a compact and varied
entertainment—brisk, direct and tricked with the
element of suspense. . . . And everyone should find
rewarding every moment of the first episode, a
grand performance of "The Cop and the Anthem,"
with Charles Laughton in the major comic role.

Archer Winsten
in the *New York Post:*

   By a process of elimination one comes back to
Charles Laughton in "The Cop and the Anthem"
as best of the lot. His performance, though pitched
to his standard of arch comedy, is clearly underlined
for laughs. . . . Marilyn Monroe, again as sleek
as she was in "The Asphalt Jungle," is a
streetwalker of stunning proportions.

With Richard Allen

Niagara

A Twentieth Century-Fox Picture (1953)

CAST

Marilyn Monroe, Joseph Cotten, Jean Peters, Casey Adams, Denis O'Dea, Richard Allan, Don Wilson, Lurene Tuttle, Russell Collins, Will Wright, Lester Matthews, Carleton Young, Sean McClory, Minerva Urecal, Nini Valera, Tom Reynolds.

CREDITS

Produced by Charles Brackett. Directed by Henry Hathaway. Written by Charles Brackett, Walter Reisch and Richard Breen. Photography by Joe MacDonald. Musical score by Sol Kaplan. Edited by Barbara McLean. In Technicolor.

SYNOPSIS.

Ray Cutler (Casey Adams) and his wife Polly (Jean Peters) go to the Canadian side of Niagara Falls on their honeymoon. At the same motel

With Joseph Cotten

With Jean Peters and Casey Adams

are George Loomis (Joseph Cotten) and his wife, Rose (Marilyn Monroe).

While visiting the Falls, Polly spots Rose kissing Ted Patrick (Richard Allan). She says nothing about the incident, even when Loomis confides to her that he believes Rose is seeing someone else. Rose and Ted want Loomis out of the way. Ted is to kill Loomis and make it look like an accident.

When Loomis turns up missing, Rose notifies the police. She collapses when she is brought in to identify a body and is taken to a hospital. Polly sees Loomis at the motel, but her husband thinks she is imagining it. Later she sees him again at the Falls, which she and Ray have revisited with friends. Finding herself alone with Loomis, Polly is terrified by the conviction that he plans to kill her. However, he helps her avoid a dangerous fall. He confides that he killed Ted in self-defense and now only wants to lose himself, and never see Rose again. Although she refuses to say whether she will or won't tell, she doesn't give him away later.

Rose flees from the hospital where she has been kept under sedation. Loomis sees her outside and pursues her into the belfry of the Carillon Tower where he strangles her.

Out with her husband and friends on a picnic, Polly again encounters

Loomis on the boat which she has boarded to get supplies—he, to escape police. When she refuses to get off, he starts the motor and the two of them speed through the water. The boat approaches the Falls, and they both realize that death is seconds away. Loomis does not want to be responsible for Polly's death, and when they come to a ledge in the river, he manages to put her on it. As she climbs to safety, the boat swerves and crashes over the Falls, carrying Loomis to his death. A helicopter rescues Polly from her precarious perch in the river.

Marilyn's eighteenth film marked the beginning of a new career for her. She was now a full-fledged star. People poured into the theaters to see her. It can truly be said that the public made Marilyn a star. Some stars are manufactured, with the studios nurturing them along in just the right vehicles for them from the start. Marilyn's unique personality and special beauty drew public notice and caused the people themselves to lift her to stardom as a result of their clamor at the boxoffice.

Marilyn sang one song in this film—"Kiss," by Lionel Newman and Haven Gillespie.

With Joseph Cotten

What the critics said about

NIAGARA

A. H. Weiler
in the *New York Times:*

Obviously ignoring the idea that there are Seven Wonders of the World, Twentieth Century-Fox has discovered two more and enhanced them with Technicolor in "Niagara," which descended on the Roxy yesterday.

For the producers are making full use of both the grandeur of the Falls and its adjacent areas as well as the grandeur that is Marilyn Monroe. The scenic effects in both cases are superb. And if a viewer cavils at the fact that the romantic melodrama enveloping the Falls and Miss Monroe is less than spectacular, then he is perfectly within his rights.

Seen from any angle, the Falls and Miss Monroe leave little to be desired by any reasonably attentive audience. . . . Perhaps Miss Monroe is not the perfect actress at this point. But neither the director nor the gentlemen who handled the cameras

appeared to be concerned with this. They have caught every possible curve both in the intimacy of the boudoir and in equally revealing tight dresses. And they have illustrated pretty concretely that she can be seductive—even when she walks.

Otis L. Guernsey, Jr.
in the *New York Herald Tribune:*

Director Henry Hathaway has put on quite a show in this "Niagara," with Marilyn Monroe, Joseph Cotten and Jean Peters sharing the billing with the natural splendors. One must admit that spectacle is the main attraction, but the script by Walter Reisch and Richard Breen is a steady, stable combination of menace and comedy relief. . . . Miss Monroe plays the kind of wife whose dress, in the words of the script, "is cut so low you can see her knees." The dress is red; the actress has very nice knees, and under Hathaway's direction she gives the kind of serpentine performance that makes the audience hate her while admiring her, which is proper for the story.

Gentlemen Prefer Blondes

A Twentieth Century-Fox Picture (1953)

CAST

Jane Russell, Marilyn Monroe, Charles Coburn, Elliott Reid, Tommy Noonan, George Winslow, Marcel Dalio, Taylor Holmes, Norma Varden, Howard Wendell, Steven Geray, Henri Letondal, Leo Mostovoy.

CREDITS

Produced by Sol C. Siegel. Directed by Howard Hawks. Screen play by Charles Lederer. Based on the musical comedy by Joseph Fields and Anita Loos. Photography by Harry J. Wild. Musical director, Lionel Newman. Dances and musical numbers staged by Jack Cole. Edited by Hugh S. Wynn. In Technicolor.

SYNOPSIS

Dorothy (Jane Russell) and Lorelei (Marilyn Monroe) work together as entertainers and are also good friends. Lorelei is engaged to wealthy Gus Esmond (Tommy Noonan). The two girls board the *Ile de France* bound for Paris, armed with a letter of credit presented Lorelei by Gus who has promised to meet her in Paris where they will be married.

Gus's father believes that Lorelei is after Gus only for his money and hires a private detective, Malone (Elliott Reid), to spy on her during the trip. When the three meet, Dorothy falls for Malone, much to the chagrin of Lorelei, who cannot understand Dorothy's indifference to men with money. Lorelei discovers that Henry Spofford, III, is on the passenger list and decides that he is the man for Dorothy. Her plans go awry when

With Jane Russell

she discovers Spofford is only a child (George Winslow). Members of the
U.S. Olympic team and many other men vie for the attentions of the
two beautiful girls, but get nowhere.

On board Lorelei meets Sir Francis Beekman (Charles Coburn), a
diamond merchant. When Beekman demonstrates to Lorelei how a python
embraces a goat, Malone snaps a picture. But Dorothy sees him, and she
and Lorelei drug him to get the picture back. When Beekman learns of
the photo, he gives Lorelei his wife's diamond tiara in appreciation for her
success in recovering it. Malone realizes that he's been had and that he has
lost Dorothy. He gathers other evidence, which, though innocent enough,
gives Gus's father ammunition to make Gus change his mind about
the marriage.

When the ship gets to Paris, Dorothy and Lorelei learn that Gus has
stopped their credit and that Lady Beekman (Norma Varden) wants her
tiara back. Dorothy and Lorelei get jobs in a night club, where Gus finds
them. The girls have learned that Lady Beekman has signed a warrant
for Lorelei's arrest. When they discover the tiara gone, Dorothy dons a
blonde wig and takes Lorelei's place in court while Lorelei works on Gus.
Malone learns that Beekman himself is the thief and recovers the tiara.
When he presents it in court the charges are dropped. Dorothy reconciles

with Malone because of his deed, while Lorelei not only redeems herself
with Gus but wins over his father (Taylor Holmes). At a double wedding
Lorelei marries Gus and Dorothy marries Malone.

Marilyn's nineteenth film was one of the classic musicals of the 1950's.
She and Jane Russell became friends during the filming of this movie,
which is evident in their performances. They worked in unison, with
neither trying to outdo the other.

Marilyn had neither sung nor danced to a great degree in any previous
film. But in this, her first starring role in a musical, she sang all of her
own numbers, as was the practice in all of her films.

Together, Marilyn and Jane sang "Two Little Girls from Little Rock" by
Jule Styne and Leo Robin and "When Love Goes Wrong" by Hoagy
Carmichael and Harold Adamson. Each girl sang "Bye Bye Baby" by Jule
Styne and Leo Robin. Marilyn's big solo was "Diamonds Are a Girl's Best
Friend" by Jule Styne and Leo Robin. Marilyn melted the screen doing
this number. Jane also did part of the same number during the courtroom
scene in which she pretended to be Lorelei. Mention should be made also
of Jane's splendid rendition of her solo number, "Ain't There Anyone Here
for Love?" by Hoagy Carmichael and Harold Adamson.

With Jane Russell and Tommy Noonan

With
Jane Russell

What the critics said about
GENTLEMEN PREFER BLONDES

Otis L. Guernsey, Jr.
in the *New York Herald Tribune:*

  With Marilyn Monroe and Jane Russell shaking everything in sight throughout a garish Technicolor production, the movie version of "Gentlemen Prefer Blondes" makes the warm weather warmer at the Roxy. Putting these two buxom pin-up girls in the same movie is merely giving two-to-one odds on a sure thing, and the payoff is big in a rousing musical. The girls have been surrounded with men and music, and they have been told to walk with that certain sway by director Howard Hawks. Singing, dancing or just staring at diamonds, these girls are irresistible and their musical is as lively as a string of firecrackers on the Fourth of July. . . . As usual, Miss Monroe looks as though she would glow in the dark, and her version of the baby-faced blonde whose eyes open for diamonds and close for kisses is always amusing as well as alluring. Miss Russell is a Juno with nylon trimmings, and she has the knack of snapping out gags with dead-pan sarcasm. They work well together in the songs and in the chase.

Miss Russell walks through the show with a long-legged stride and Miss Monroe limits herself down to a lazy amble, but somehow they always seem to come out even.

Archer Winsten
in the *New York Post:*

  The picture, not content with good-enough, broadens an already broad theme, thereby coming too close to burlesque for constant satisfaction. But when you come right down to it, what more can you want than Marilyn Monroe under constant command to be sexy and Jane Russell trying to get her traditional share of the attention. The girls wear form-fitting thises and thats, revealing native talents long celebrated in pin-ups, traveling compartment conversations, and legend of the cinema world. And just as if those forms couldn't attract sufficient attention, they are gyrated in fashions that must have originated long before Man climbed into his first tree. . . . As entertainment, "Gentlemen Prefer Blondes" is gay visually and kinetically, comparatively philosophical in its songs, and perhaps slightly heavy-handed in its preoccupation with that one method a girl uses to procure more "best friends."

With George Winslow

With Jane Russell and Elliott Reed

With Jane Russell

With Lauren Bacall

How to Marry
a Millionaire

With Betty Grable and Lauren Bacall

A Twentieth Century-Fox Picture (1953)

CAST

Marilyn Monroe, Betty Grable, Lauren Bacall, William Powell, David Wayne, Rory Calhoun, Cameron Mitchell, Alex D'Arcy, Fred Clark, George Dunn, Percy Helton.

CREDITS

Produced by Nunnally Johnson. Directed by Jean Negulesco. Screen play by Nunnally Johnson. Based on plays by Zoe Akins and Dale Eunson and Katherine Albert. Photography by Joe MacDonald. Musical direction by Alfred Newman. Incidental music by Cyril Mockridge. Edited by Louis Loeffler. In CinemaScope and Technicolor.

SYNOPSIS

Three models, Pola Debevoise (Marilyn Monroe), Loco Dempsey (Betty Grable) and Schatze Page (Lauren Bacall), pool their resources to rent an expensive penthouse apartment in New York, each girl hoping to trap a millionaire husband for herself.

Tom Brookman (Cameron Mitchell) helps Loco with groceries one day and meets and falls in love with Schatze. But she spurns him, thinking he

With David Wayne

With Cameron Mitchell, Betty Grable
and Lauren Bacall

is poor. Unknown to them all, he is in reality a millionaire. The girls are
nearly broke when Loco introduces them to an oil tycoon, J. D. Hanley
(William Powell), who becomes interested in Schatze.

Loco takes a trip with wealthy and married Waldo Brewster (Fred
Clark), under the impression that they are going to a convention in Maine.
Once at his lodge, she realizes they will be alone and is set to return to
New York when she comes down with the measles. A forest ranger
named Eben (Rory Calhoun) comes into her life, and they fall in love.

Pola leaves by plane to meet J. Stewart Merrill (Alex D'Arcy) in Atlantic
City, thinking he wants her to meet his mother. But because she refuses
to wear glasses in public to correct her nearsightedness, she gets on the
wrong plane. On board she meets Freddie Denmark (David Wayne), the
landlord of her penthouse apartment, who is on his way to find his tax
accountant because of whom he is in trouble with the revenue department.

Schatze, left alone and without money, agrees to marry the wealthy
Hanley. Loco arrives with Eben on the wedding day. Pola also turns up
with a battered Freddie. He had turned his conniving accountant over
to authorities after a fight, and then had married Pola.

Tom Brookman is there, too, and Hanley realizes that he is the man
Schatze really loves. They call off the wedding, Schatze deciding that love
is preferable to money. The three couples go to a diner, where all faint
when Tom pulls out an enormous wad of bills to pay the check.

Marilyn's twentieth film was her first in CinemaScope. Incidentally, this
was the second CinemaScope film ever made, the first being "The Robe."

Marilyn co-starred here with Betty Grable, who had been Fox's leading
star for years. Prophets of fireworks had to eat their forecasts, for Marilyn
responded in kind to Betty's friendliness.

This film marked David Wayne's last movie appearance with Marilyn.
He made four pictures with her—more than any other actor.

With William Powell and Lauren Bacall

With Alex D'Arcy

With Alex D'Arcy

With Lauren Bacall
and David Wayne

With Betty Grable
and William Powell (far right)

What the critics said about
HOW TO MARRY A MILLIONAIRE

Otis L. Guernsey, Jr.
in the *New York Herald Tribune:*

The big question, "How does Marilyn Monroe look stretched across a broad screen?" is easily answered. If you insisted on sitting in the front row, you would probably feel as though you were being smothered in baked Alaska. From any normal vantage point, though, her magnificent proportions are as appealing as ever, and her stint as a dead-pan comedienne is as nifty as her looks. Playing a near-sighted charmer who won't wear her glasses when men are around, she bumps into the furniture and reads books upside down with a limpid guile that nearly melts the screen.

Archer Winsten
in the *New York Post:*

"How to Marry a Millionaire," CinemaScoped simultaneously at the Globe and Loew's State Theatres, is an extremely entertaining film, and it would be that, like its predecessor, "The Robe," no matter what its condition of width, height, and depth. . . . Monroe is a comparative innocent who smiles at anything in hopes it might be masculine. Since she doesn't want to be seen wearing glasses, she can never be sure. But her shape, which does not seem to be deteriorating in any way, is sufficient guarantee that a goodly percentage of human beings in her vicinity will turn out to be male and virile. . . . It is particularly noteworthy that Miss Monroe has developed more than a small amount of comedy polish of the foot-in-mouth type.

Kate Cameron
in the *New York Daily News:*

The picture, in Technicolor, is adorned by a beauteous trio of feminine stars who play their roles so smartly and ingratiatingly that they keep the audience in a state of hilarity all through the running of the comedy. Betty Grable, Lauren Bacall and Marilyn Monroe give off the quips and cracks, generously supplied by Nunnally Johnson, with a naturalness that adds to their strikingly humorous effect, making the film the funniest comedy of the year.

Betty Grable, Rory Calhoun, Lauren Bacall,
Cameron Mitchell, Marilyn, and David Wayne

With Robert Mitchum

A Twentieth Century-Fox Picture (1954)

CAST

Robert Mitchum, Marilyn Monroe, Rory Calhoun, Tommy Rettig, Murvyn Vye, Douglas Spencer, Ed Hinton, Don Beddoe, Claire Andre, Jack Mather, Edmund Cobb, Will Wright, Jarma Lewis, Hal Baylor.

CREDITS

Produced by Stanley Rubin. Directed by Otto Preminger. Screen play by Frank Fenton. From a story by Louis Lantz. Photography by Joseph LaShelle. Musical score by Cyril Mockridge. Choreography by Jack Cole. Edited by Louis Loeffler. In CinemaScope and Technicolor.

SYNOPSIS

In the 1875 Northwest, widower Matt Calder (Robert Mitchum), comes to town, where his ten-year-old son Mark (Tommy Rettig) is waiting for him. He has served a term in prison for shooting a man in the back, even though he shot the man only to keep him from murdering a friend. Mark has now been sent to join his father, who has bought a farm for them.

Mark has made the acquaintance of Kay (Marilyn Monroe), a saloon

River *of* No Return

With Rory Calhoun

singer, while waiting for his father. Calder thanks Kay for her kindness to
his boy, and father and son depart for their farm.

One day, Calder sees Kay and gambler Harry Weston (Rory Calhoun)
in trouble on a raft in the river near his home. He helps them ashore
and learns that Weston is in a hurry to get to town to register a gold claim.
So eager is he that he steals his rescuer's only horse, and leaving his girl
behind as well, rides away.

The predicament of those left is deepened by the fact that Indians are
on a rampage and are due to attack the farm at any moment. The only
way left to get to town is by the river, so Calder, Kay and Mark set out
on the raft. Calder is determined to take revenge on Weston for leaving
them to the mercy of the Indians. Kay knows this and in a burst of anger
mentions Calder's prison term. Mark is stunned and refuses to believe
his father's explanation of the killing.

As the trip progresses, the three encounter danger from outlaws, Indians
and the treacherous river. Kay finds herself falling in love with Calder as
she sees what a thoughtful and unselfish man he really is. Finally,
having successfully brought the raft through the rough waters, they arrive
at the town.

Kay finds Weston and asks him not to fight with Calder but refuses to
take up with him again. Weston spots Calder and fires at him, though
Calder is unarmed. Kay tries to fight Weston but he pushes her away.
Seeing what is happening, Mark is forced to shoot Weston in the back.

Thus he comes to understand how it was that his father had been forced to kill.

There is still a gulf of misunderstanding between Kay and Calder, however, and Kay goes off to get a job singing in a saloon. But Calder has other ideas. He seeks her out where she is holding forth and carries her off. Thus Kay is persuaded to embark upon a new life with Calder and Mark.

It was inevitable that even Marilyn would wind up in a western. In her twenty-first film she competed with the beautiful scenery and won.

Marilyn sang four numbers in this film: "The River of No Return," "I'm Gonna File My Claim," "One Silver Dollar," and "Down in the Meadow," by Ken Darby and Lionel Newman.

With Robert Mitchum and Tommy Rettig

With Robert Mitchum

With Robert Mitchum

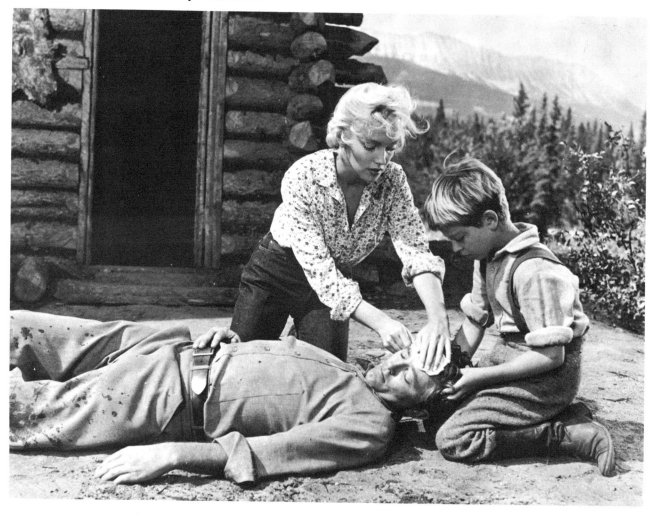

With Robert Mitchum and Tommy Rettig

What the critics said about
RIVER OF NO RETURN

Bosley Crowther
in the *New York Times:*

It is a toss-up whether the scenery or the adornment of Marilyn Monroe is the feature of greater attraction in "River of No Return," the Twentieth Century-Fox outdoor drama that showed up yesterday on the Roxy's wide screen. The mountainous scenery is spectacular, but so, in her own way, is Miss Monroe. The patron's preference, if any, probably will depend upon which he's interested in.

Certainly Scriptwriter Frank Fenton has done the best he could to arrange for a fairly equal balance of nature and Miss Monroe. . . . Director Otto Preminger has thrown all the grandeur and menace of these features upon the eye-filling CinemaScope screen. . . . But Mr. Mitchum's and the audience's attention is directed to Miss Monroe through frequent and liberal posing of her in full and significant views.

Archer Winsten
in the *New York Post:*

Speaking generally, the scenery is beyond reproach, and CinemaScope here finds something to get its broad span of teeth into. The outdoor action on the river is dramatically very powerful. Mr. Mitchum and the other males seem at home among the mountains and trees, and that leaves only Miss Monroe as the picture's vibrant question mark. There is something at once incongruous and strangely stimulating in Miss Monroe's dazzled and dazzling antics in the surroundings of nature. She herself is a leading representative of the natural instinct mentioned previously, and she is also, by reason of the artificial aspect of her coloring and makeup, in opposition to nature. This creates a kind of tension, not too easily defined, but very easily translated into publicity, popularity, and public interest.

With Robert Mitchum

There's No Business Like Show Business

With Donald O'Conner

A Twentieth Century-Fox Picture (1954)

CAST

Ethel Merman, Donald O'Connor, Marilyn Monroe, Dan Dailey, Johnnie Ray, Mitzi Gaynor, Richard Eastham, Hugh O'Brian, Frank McHugh, Rhys Williams, Lee Patrick, Eve Miller, Robin Raymond, Lyle Talbot, George Melford, Alvy Moore, Chick Chandler.

CREDITS

Produced by Sol C. Siegel. Directed by Walter Lang. Screen play by Phoebe and Henry Ephron. From a story by Lamar Trotti. Photography by Leon Shamroy. Music supervised and conducted by Alfred Newman and Lionel Newman. Dances and musical numbers staged by Robert Alton. Edited by Robert Simpson. In CinemaScope and Color by DeLuxe.

SYNOPSIS

Molly and Terry Donahue (Ethel Merman and Dan Dailey) bring up their three children in show business, the family forming an act billed as The Five Donahues. The three young Donahues are Tim (Donald O'Connor), Katy (Mitzi Gaynor) and Steve (Johnnie Ray).

Steve quits the act to study for the priesthood. Tim meets Vicky (Marilyn Monroe) at a night club where she is a hat-check girl and sees her do a song when her agent brings a producer to meet her. The Four Donahues get a booking in a Florida hotel, where Tim discovers that Vicky is also on the bill. He talks his family into doing something else so that Vicky can do their "Heat Wave" number, which sets Molly against Vicky. When

(Both pages) Marilyn's controversial "Heat Wave" number

Vicky convinces Tim and Katy to go into a Broadway show with her, Molly and Terry go on their own successfully.

Katy becomes interested in Charley Gibbs (Hugh O'Brian), lyric writer for the show. Tim, who has fallen in love with Vicky, mistakenly thinks she is two-timing him with the show's producer, Lew Harris (Richard Eastham). On opening night he gets drunk and is hurt in a car accident. Molly goes on in his place with Katy, and Terry goes to see him at the hospital. Tim is not badly hurt and Terry berates him for getting drunk on opening night, finally hitting him and leaving in a huff. Later when he returns with Molly, Tim has gone and they are unable to find him anywhere.

Terry begins to brood, becoming so morose that he even gives up performing. Molly continues in the show with Katy, although she avoids

Vicky, whom she blames for Tim's disappearance. Katy, who doesn't share her mother's bitterness against Vicky, marries Charley Gibbs.

Molly tries to get Terry to do an act for the Actors' Fund at the Hippodrome Theatre, which is going to be torn down soon, but Terry refuses. Katy determines to use the occasion as a means for getting her mother together with Vicky. The two women meet, and Vicky tells Molly that she still loves Tim and that he had no reason to be jealous of Harris. Molly believes her and they bury the hatchet.

Steve, now an army chaplain, arrives backstage. Molly goes on to do her number. Tim, who has joined the Navy, arrives backstage also, and Molly sees him from her position on stage. When Terry joins the happy reunion, the original Five Donahues go on stage for a number. Vicky gets into the act, too, standing beside Tim while the six sing "There's No Business Like Show Business."

This was a film tribute to composer Irving Berlin, and Marilyn's twenty-second film. She sang three numbers in the picture: "After You Get What You Want You Don't Want It," "Heat Wave," and "Lazy."

(Above) Marilyn singing "After You Get What You Want,
You Don't Want It"

Facing page:
(Top) With Donald O'Conner and Mitzi Gaynor
(Bottom) With Ethel Merman and Johnny Ray

What the critics said about
THERE'S NO BUSINESS LIKE SHOW BUSINESS

Kate Cameron
in the *New York Daily News:*
   "There's No Business Like Show Business" is full
to overflowing with entertainment material. . . .
Photographed in DeLuxe Color, it is a star-studded
production with an Irving Berlin score that gives
the film rhythm, bounce and a pleasant nostalgic
quality. . . . Marilyn stars in three specialty
numbers amusingly, as she does a comic burlesque
of the sexy singer of naughty songs.

Frank Quinn
in the *New York Daily Mirror:*
   Marilyn Monroe, who shocks Donald out of
show business and into uniform, is given a trio of
tunes, sung and performed in her trademarked
sexy manner. . . . All are sizzling. . . . "There's
No Business Like Show Business" is a big
extravaganza, colorfully bright and melodic. Just
lots of plain, wonderful sentiment.

Bosley Crowther
in the *New York Times:*
   When it comes to spreading talent, Miss Gaynor
has the jump on Miss Monroe, whose wriggling
and squirming to "Heat Wave" and "Lazy" are
embarrassing to behold.

The Seven Year Itch

A Twentieth Century-Fox Picture (1955)

CAST

   Marilyn Monroe, Tom Ewell, Evelyn Keyes, Sonny Tufts, Robert Strauss, Oscar Homolka, Marguerite Chapman, Victor Moore, Roxanne, Donald MacBride, Carolyn Jones, Butch Bernard, Doro Merande, Dorothy Ford.

CREDITS

   Produced by Charles K. Feldman and Billy Wilder. Directed by Billy Wilder. Screen play by Billy Wilder and George Axelrod. Based on the play by George Axelrod. Photography by Milton Krasner. Music by Alfred Newman. Edited by Hugh S. Fowler. In CinemaScope and Color by DeLuxe.

SYNOPSIS

   Richard Sherman (Tom Ewell) and his wife Helen (Evelyn Keyes) have been married for seven years. While he remains in New York on business, Helen and their son Ricky (Butch Bernard) go off to a resort for a summer vacation.
   The apartment above has been sublet to The Girl (Marilyn Monroe), a TV model. When she forgets her front door key, she presses Sherman's

buzzer and he lets her into the building. Alone, he imagines love affairs with women he has met.

When The Girl accidentally knocks a tomato plant onto Sherman's terrace, he invites her down for a drink, indulging in fantasies about making love to her while he is waiting. She comes in, explaining that she feels safe with married men. He makes a clumsy pass while they are at the piano but both fall off the bench. He stammers an apology, but she pretends it is nothing.

When The Girl returns to her apartment, Sherman envisions her telling everyone that he is a masher. In his fantasy, she first tells a plumber (Victor Moore), who has extracted her toe caught in the faucet of her bathtub while she is bathing. The plumber spreads the news while The Girl herself warns people about him over television. He imagines Helen's finding out and retaliating by having an affair with Tom MacKenzie (Sonny Tufts), an acquaintance of theirs whom he dislikes intensely and who is also at the resort. Finally he decides to put an end to visions and asks The Girl out to dinner and a movie. On the way home, she stops on a subway grating, enjoying the cool breeze billowing up from it.

The Girl tells him that she does a toothpaste commercial and shows Sherman that she has sweet breath with a kiss. At his apartment, she falls

With Tom Ewell

With Tom Ewell

in love with the air conditioning and asks Sherman to let her sleep there. He reluctantly gives her the bedroom while he sleeps in the living room. Again his imagination runs riot. He pictures The Girl and the building janitor, Kruhulik (Robert Strauss), in on a plot to blackmail him and Helen finally murdering him.

In the harsh light of morning, Sherman expresses his doubts that any woman would be jealous over him. She realizes that his ego is suffering and declares that she finds him more attractive than many handsome men she knows. Later when she is in the kitchen, Tom MacKenzie arrives. Helen has asked him to bring something of Ricky's back to the resort.

All of Sherman's jealous fantasies about Helen and Tom run through his mind, and he knocks Tom unconscious. Kruhulik comes in and carries him away. Sherman decides he'd better join Helen and offers The Girl his air-conditioned apartment while he's gone.

The Girl gives Sherman a grateful kiss which communicates her conviction that he's a decent sort. She also means to say that she sincerely likes the poor boob. Overwhelmed, Sherman rushes out of the house. The Girl yells after him, throwing down the shoes he has forgotten to put on, and he heads for the railroad station.

Her twenty-third film featured Marilyn in another of her subtle performances. Although playing a dumb blonde, she suggested a depth of character not immediately apparent in the script.

Marilyn's personal life was in turmoil while she was making this film. She and her second husband, baseball player Joe DiMaggio, were in the process of divorce.

What the critics said about
THE SEVEN YEAR ITCH

Bosley Crowther
in the *New York Times:*

Miss Monroe brings a special personality and a certain physical something or other to the film that may not be exactly what the playwright ordered but which definitely conveys an idea.

From the moment she steps into the picture, in a garment that drapes her shapely form as though she had been skillfully poured into it, the famous screen star with the silver-blonde tresses and the ingenuously wide-eyed stare emanates one suggestion. And that suggestion rather dominates the film. It is—well, why define it? Miss Monroe clearly plays the title role.

Philip Strassberg
in the *New York Daily Mirror:*

This is the picture every red-blooded American male has been awaiting ever since the publication of the tease photos showing the wind lifting Marilyn Monroe's skirt above her shapely gams.

It was worth waiting for. "The Seven Year Itch" is another example of cinema ingenuity in transplanting a stage success to celluloid. . . . Tom Ewell, who reaped critical acclaim in the legit show and won over other contenders for the role in the movie and La Monroe deserve most of the credit for carrying off the comedy coup. . . . Ewell is an extremely funny fellow whose pliable features and ungainly gait add to his natural humor. He's been kicking around for a long time and deserves this Hollywood success for his talents. And when you can "steal" a picture from La Monroe's architecture—it's a tremendous accomplishment.

This isn't to detract from Marilyn's status as a fine comedienne. Her pouting delivery, puckered lips—the personification of this decade's glamour—make her one of Hollywood's top attractions, which she again proves here as the not too bright model.

(Both pictures)
with Tom Ewell

With Don Murray

Bus Stop

A Twentieth Century-Fox Picture (1956)

CAST

Marilyn Monroe, Don Murray, Arthur O'Connell, Betty Field, Eileen Heckart, Robert Bray, Hope Lange, Hans Conried, Casey Adams, Henry Slate, Terry Kellman, Linda Brace, Greta Thyssen, Helen Mayon, Lucille Knox, Kate MacKenna.

CREDITS

Produced by Buddy Adler. Directed by Joshua Logan. Screen play by George Axelrod. Based on the play by William Inge. Photography by Milton Krasner. Musical score by Alfred Newman and Cyril Mockridge. Edited by William Reynolds. In CinemaScope and Color by DeLuxe.

SYNOPSIS

A young and innocent cowboy, Bo Decker (Don Murray), is brought from his Montana ranch by his friend Virgil (Arthur O'Connell) to a rodeo in Phoenix, Arizona.

At the Blue Dragon café in Phoenix, Bo discovers Cherie (Marilyn Monroe), a singer of uncertain virtue. He is indignant at the inattention of patrons during her number and bullies them into a respectful silence. The kiss she gives him in appreciation determines him then and there

to make her his wife. Virgil, who knew her, is dismayed when Bo confides his plans to him.

Bo bursts into Cherie's room in the morning, waking her up to tell her they are going to be married that day. Her reaction is one of total bafflement. Later she and her friend Vera (Eileen Heckart), a waitress, attend the rodeo in which Bo is participating. When she realizes that Bo actually intends to bring a minister to marry them, she flees from the grounds, determined to get out of town. Virgil loans her money to get a bus to Los Angeles, but Bo finds her and forces her to get on the bus to Montana with him and Virgil.

On the bus, Cherie confides in a young girl named Elma (Hope Lange), revealing, in addition to her current predicament, details of her past; her ambition to go to Hollywood, the men she has known, and her disillusionment with life.

When the bus comes to a stop at Grace's Diner, Elma takes Cherie inside while Bo is asleep and explains to Grace (Betty Field) about the kidnapping. The passengers are informed that the road is blocked and that they must stay at the diner until it is cleared. Carl (Robert Bray), the bus driver, is also told about Cherie's plight.

When Bo and Virgil come into the café, Bo sees that Cherie has taken her suitcase off the bus and realizes that she is planning to escape. Nothing daunted, he slings Cherie on his back to take her to the nearest minister, warning protesting witnesses not to interfere. But Carl stops Bo and a battle ensues in which the driver is victor.

Bo tells Virgil that he cannot face Cherie after his defeat and goes off to sit in the bus by himself. He returns to the diner in the morning, where Virgil points out that people will never respect or listen to him if he persists in acting the brute. Chastened, Bo apologizes to everyone for his actions and asks Cherie's forgiveness for all he has done. Alluding to her questionable past, Cherie assures him he's better off without her.

Then a call comes through that the road is cleared, Bo asks Cherie if he can kiss her goodbye. The kiss affects her more than she had bargained for. Encouraged, Bo renewes his suit, stressing that what she did before she met him doesn't matter. Tearfully, Cherie agrees to marry him. Bo tells Virgil, who has come to see Cherie in a new light. When Bo and Cherie board the bus to Montana, Virgil announces his intention to remain, pointing out that since Bo is going to be a married man, he won't be needing a guardian.

Marilyn's twenty-fourth film offered, in the opinion of many, her greatest performance. After "The Seven Year Itch" she had left Hollywood and studied with Lee and Paula Strasberg at the Actors Studio in New York. Her performance in this film was doubtless profoundly affected by what.she learned there.

Marilyn singing "That Old Black Magic"

(Both pages) With Don Murray

What the critics said about
BUS STOP

Bosley Crowther
in the *New York Times:*

Hold onto your chairs, everybody, and get set for a rattling surprise. Marilyn Monroe has finally proved herself an actress in "Bus Stop." She and the picture are swell!

This piece of professional information may seem both implausible and absurd to those who have gauged the lady's talents by her performances in such films as "Niagara," "Gentlemen Prefer Blondes" and even "The Seven Year Itch," wherein her magnetism was put forth by other qualities than her histrionic skill. And it may also cause some skepticism on the part of those who saw the play by William Inge, from which the film is lifted, and remember Kim Stanley in the role.

But all you have to do to test our comment is to hop around to the Roxy, where the film, produced by Twentieth Century-Fox and directed by Joshua Logan, opened yesterday. If you don't find Miss Monroe a downright Duse, you'll find her a dilly, anyhow.

For the striking fact is that Mr. Logan has got her to do a great deal more than wiggle and pout and pop her big eyes and play the synthetic vamp in this film. He has got her to be the beat-up B-girl of Mr. Inge's play, even down to the Ozark accent and the look of pellagra about her skin.

He has got her to be the tinseled floozie, the semi-moronic doll who is found in a Phoenix clip-joint by a cowboy of equally limited brains and is hotly pursued by this suitor to a snow-bound bus stop in the Arizona wilds. And, what's most important, he has got her to light the small flame of dignity that sputters pathetically in this chippie and to make a rather moving sort of her.

This may not sound too stimulating to those who prefer their Miss Monroe looking healthy and without anything flaming inside her except a mad desire. But don't think because the little lady creates a real character in this film she or it are lacking in vitality, humor or attractiveness.

William K. Zinsser
in the *New York Herald Tribune:*

Eighteen months ago Marilyn Monroe quit Hollywood and came East to study "serious" acting. Now she is back on the screen—in "Bus Stop," at the Roxy—and everybody can see what the "new" Marilyn is like.

Actually there was never anything wrong with the old Marilyn. She had certain skills no amount of teaching could improve. But she never had a role with any depth.

In "Bus Stop" she has a wonderful role, and she plays it with a mixture of humor and pain that is very touching. This is also the special genius of of the movie. One minute it is uproariously funny, the next minute tender and fragile, and somehow director Joshua Logan preserves the delicate balance.

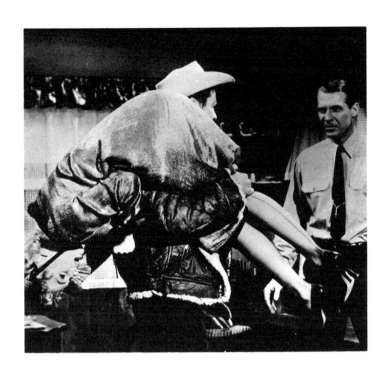

The Prince and the Showgirl

With Laurence Olivier

A Warner Bros. Presentation of a Film by Marilyn Monroe Productions, Inc. and L.O.P. Ltd. (1957)

CAST

Marilyn Monroe, Laurence Olivier, Sybil Thorndike, Richard Wattis, Jeremy Spenser, Esmond Knight, Paul Hardwick, Rosamund Greenwood, Aubrey Dexter, Maxine Audley, Harold Goodwin, Andrea Malandrinos, Jean Kent, Daphne Anderson, Gillian Owen, Vera Day, Margot Lister, Charles Victor, David Horne, Dennis Edwards, Gladys Henson.

CREDITS

Produced and directed by Laurence Olivier. Executive producer, Milton H. Greene. Screen play by Terence Rattigan. From a play by Terence Rattigan. Photography by Jack Cardiff. Music by Richard Addinsell. Dances arranged by William Chappell. Edited by Jack Harris. In Technicolor.

SYNOPSIS

Grand Duke Charles (Laurence Olivier), Prince Regent of Carpathia, visits London in 1911 for the coronation of George V. With him are his

young son King Nicholas (Jeremy Spenser), and his mother-in-law, the Queen Dowager (Sybil Thorndike).

The Prince Regent sees American showgirl Elsie Marina (Marilyn Monroe) in a stage show and invites her to dinner at the Carpathian Embassy. When Elsie arrives, he begins to make amorous advances which she successfully wards off.

Nicholas bursts into the room and demands to know' why one of his friends has been arrested in Carpathia. His father replies by ordering him back to his room and having him locked in. The Queen Dowager is the next to meet Elsie, who finds it amazing that neither she nor Nicholas were embarrassed at seeing her there.

While the Prince Regent wearies of making unsuccessful passes, Elsie gets drunk and falls asleep. Angrily, he puts her in a bedroom to sleep it off, and leaves. In the morning when she wakes up, she realizes that she has fallen in love. The object of her affections, however, only wants her out of his life.

Elsie learns that Nicholas plans to wrest control of the government from his father now rather than wait until he becomes of age eighteen months hence. Having become lady-in-waiting to the Queen Dowager for the coronation, Elsie mediates between father and son. Nicholas's terms for not assuming the throne prematurely center around an immediate general election. This the Prince Regent is dead against. He fears that the Kaiser will come to power in his country if such an election is held.

In any case, Elsie manages to accomplish her twin goals of reconciling the King and Prince Regent and winning the heart of the latter. The Prince Regent must return to his country, but in a year and a half—when Nicholas is to become a full-fledged king—he will return for her. Elsie happily promises to wait for him.

Marilyn's twenty-fifth film was made by her own company which she set up with Milton Greene. The star was now in her early thirties, and like most pretty women, she had become beautiful after thirty. Never was she more so than in this film.

With Sybil Thorndike

With Sybil Thorndike

What the critics said about
THE PRINCE AND THE SHOWGIRL

Archer Winsten
in the *New York Post:*

Marilyn Monroe . . . has never seemed more in command of herself as person and comedienne. She manages to make her laughs without sacrificing the real Marilyn to play-acting. This, of course, is something one can expect from great, talented and practiced performers. It comes as a most pleasant surprise from Marilyn Monroe, who has been half-actress, half-sensation.

Alton Cook
in the *New York World-Telegram and Sun:*

The unpredictable waverings of Marilyn Monroe's acting promise soar to a triumphant peak in "The Prince and the Showgirl" at Radio City Music Hall. The movie is also a comic delight, matching the surprise bestowed upon us by Marilyn.

As her co-star and director, Laurence Olivier brings out qualities none of her films ever summoned. She is captivatingly kittenish in her infectious mirth. Her love scenes are played as a girlish game. She romps through slapstick and turns solemn moments into part of her fun.

William K. Zinsser
in the *New York Herald Tribune:*

"The Prince and the Showgirl" is great fun if you don't take it seriously. Certainly its author doesn't. Terence Rattigan is just playing a game, amusing us for two hours, and the actors enjoy the charade immensely. They try to look earnest but a twinkle in the eye betrays them.

In the case of Olivier, the twinkle must fight its way through a thick monocle to reach the outside world and it does. This is a performance of rich, subtle humor. . . . Marilyn's role has no such fine shadings. This is a dumb, affable showgirl and nothing more, and Miss Monroe goes through the motions with mirth, childish innocence, squeals of pleasure, pouts of annoyance, eyes big as golf balls, and many a delighted toss of her rounded surfaces.

With Laurence Olivier

Some Like It Hot

*A United Artists Release   A Mirisch Company Presentation
of an Ashton Picture* (1959)

CAST

Marilyn Monroe, Tony Curtis, Jack Lemmon, George Raft, Pat O'Brien,
Joe E. Brown, Nehemiah Persoff, Joan Shawlee, Billy Gray, George
Stone, Dave Barry, Mike Mazurki, Harry Wilson, Edward G. Robinson, Jr.

CREDITS

Produced and directed by Billy Wilder. Screen play by Billy Wilder
and I. A. L. Diamond. Suggested from a story by R. Thoeren and M.
Logan. Photography by Charles Lang, Jr. Background music by Adolph
Deutsch. Songs supervised by Matty Malneck. Edited by Arthur Schmidt.

SYNOPSIS

In 1929 Chicago, Spats Colombo (George Raft) and his gang massacre
a rival gang in a garage. Two musicians, Joe (Tony Curtis) and Jerry
(Jack Lemmon), see it and flee. To escape the gang, they dress as

(Both pages)
With Jack Lemmon

Jack Lemmon and Tony Curtis

women and get jobs with an all-girl orchestra. Joe calls himself Josephine and Jerry calls himself Daphne.

The orchestra takes a train to play an engagement in Florida. On board, the two men have a hard time keeping cool with all the beautiful girls around, especially during a drinking party in a berth. Joe falls in love with Sugar (Marilyn Monroe), a ukulele player and vocalist with the band. Sugar also likes alcohol and millionaires.

Once in Florida, Jerry meets millionaire Osgood Fielding (Joe E. Brown).

Of course, Jerry is still dressed as Daphne, and Osgood proceeds to pursue
Daphne. Joe wants to make good with Sugar but knows that he needs a
wealthy front. While Jerry keeps Osgood on shore, Joe makes use of
Osgood's yacht.

Joe, with his woman's garb shed, meets Sugar and pretends to be an oil
magnate. He tells her that he has a complex about women and cannot
get excited about them. She accompanies him to the yacht, vowing
that she will cure him of his complex.

The boys think they are safe until Spats and his gang come to Florida to
attend a gangsters' convention. They spot Joe and Jerry, who hide under
a table at a gangland dinner. When Spats is killed there by a rival gang,

With Jack Lemmon

police arrive. Joe grabs Sugar and with Jerry and Osgood leaves in Osgood's motor launch. Joe tells Sugar all, but she decides he is for her even though he doesn't have money. Jerry tells Osgood that he is really a man and that marriage is impossible, but Osgood, unperturbed, retorts, "Nobody's perfect."

Marilyn's twenty-sixth film was an uproarious comedy. It will remain through the years as a comedy classic

Marilyn sang three songs in the film: "I'm Through with Love" by Gus Kahn, Matty Malneck and F. Livingston; "I Wanna Be Loved by You" by Bert Kalmar, Harry Ruby and Herbert Stothart; and "Running Wild" by Joe Gray and Leo Worth.

With Tony Curtis

What the critics said about
SOME LIKE IT HOT

A. H. Weiler
in the *New York Times*:

Mr. Wilder, abetted by such equally proficient operatives as Marilyn Monroe, Jack Lemmon and Tony Curtis, surprisingly has developed a completely unbelievable plot into a broad farce in which authentically comic action vies with snappy and sophisticated dialogue. . . . As the band's somewhat simple singer-ukulele player, Miss Monroe, whose figure simply cannot be overlooked, contributes more assets than the obvious ones to this madcap romp. As a pushover for gin and the tonic effect of saxophone players, she sings a couple of whispery old numbers ("Running Wild" and "I Wanna Be Loved by You") and also proves to be the epitome of a dumb blonde and a talented comedienne.

Hift
in *Variety*:

"Some Like It Hot," directed in masterly style by Billy Wilder, is probably the funniest picture of recent memory. It's a whacky, clever, farcical comedy that starts off like a firecracker and keeps on throwing off lively sparks till the very end. . . . To coin a phrase, Marilyn has never looked better. Her performance as "Sugar," the fuzzy blonde who likes saxophone players and men with glasses has a deliciously naive quality. She's a comedienne with that combination of sex appeal and timing that just can't be beat.

Archer Winsten
in the *New York Post*:

To get down to cases, Marilyn does herself proud, giving a performance of such intrinsic quality that you begin to believe she's only being herself and it is herself who fits into that distant period and this picture so well.

Let's Make Love

A Twentieth Century-Fox Picture (1960)   With Yves Montand

CAST

Marilyn Monroe, Yves Montand, Tony Randall, Frankie Vaughan, Wilfrid Hyde White, David Burns, Michael David, Mara Lynn, Dennis King, Jr., Joe Besser, Madge Kennedy, Ray Foster, Mike Mason, John Craven, Harry Chesire. Guest Stars: Bing Crosby, Milton Berle, Gene Kelly.

CREDITS

Produced by Jerry Wald. Directed by George Cukor. Written for the screen by Norman Krasna. Additional material by Hal Kanter. Photography by Daniel L. Fapp. Music by Lionel Newman. Musical numbers staged by Jack Cole. Edited by David Bretherton. In CinemaScope and Color by DeLuxe.

SYNOPSIS

Jean-Marc Clement (Yves Montand), a billionaire, learns from his lawyer, Wales (Wilfrid Hyde White), and his public relations director,

Alex Coffman (Tony Randall), that he is to be one of the prominent people satirized in an upcoming off-Broadway revue.

Clement and Coffman go to the theater, where they see Amanda Dell (Marilyn Monroe) rehearsing a song. The director, thinking Clement is an actor, hires him to play the part of himself in the revue. Clement accepts because he wants to see more of Amanda. Unaware of his identity, Amanda tells him that she is not impressed with wealthy men, especially Clement. The billionaire's rival seems to be Tony Danton (Frankie Vaughan), singer and comic in the show.

Wales learns that Clement Enterprises owns the theatre and plans to close it down. When Coffman learns about it, he thinks Clement is responsible; whereupon he gets drunk and tells him off. But Clement explains that he has no intention of closing the theater. On the contrary, he plans to put money in the show through Wales and marry Amanda as well.

Clement gets three show business celebrities (Bing Crosby, Gene Kelly, and Milton Berle to do these guest stints in the film) to teach him how to sing, dance, and be a comic. Wales pretends to be the backer of the revue. When Danton learns that Clement is going to do a song for Wales,

With Frankie Vaughan

With Yves Montand

With Frankie Vaughan

he gets angry and threatens to quit. Amanda goes out to dinner with Clement so that Danton can do the number.

Amanda tells Clement that she tricked him. He believes the confession means that she loves him. He tells her who he really is and asks her to marry him, but she thinks he's lying.

Clement hits upon a plan. He gets an injunction to stop the show and then agrees to go with Amanda to reason with the owner of the theater. When they get to his office, she realizes he really is Clement and flees in an elevator. He brings the elevator back up and kisses her as she protests and tries to fight him off. Her resistance is short-lived, however. It dawns on her that she loves him despite his deception and billions, and she melts into his arms.

Marilyn's twenty-seventh film was a light comedy which teamed her with Montand from France and Vaughan from England. Marilyn sang four numbers in the film: "My Heart Belongs to Daddy" by Cole Porter, and three songs written by Sammy Cahn and James Van Heusen, "Let's Make Love," "Incurably Romantic," and "Specialization."

(Both pages) Marilyn sings
"My Heart Belongs to Daddy"

What the critics said about
LET'S MAKE LOVE

Justin Gilbert
in the *New York Daily Mirror:*

Miss Monroe, basically a first-rate comedienne, doesn't have a single bright line. Of course, the famous charms are in evidence. . . . Miss Monroe projects in a couple of musical offerings, including "My Heart Belongs to Daddy," and another.

Alton Cook
in the *New York World-Telegram and Sun:*

Marilyn Monroe is geared for some of the loudest laughter of her life in "Let's Make Love." . . . It is a gay, preposterous and completely delightful romp. . . . Marilyn actually dares comparison with Mary Martin by singing "My Heart Belongs to Daddy" in her first scene. The night I saw it, the audience broke into the picture with applause.

The Misfits

(Both pages)
With Montgomery Clift and Clark Gable

*A United Artists Release. A Seven Arts Productions
Presentation of a John Huston Production (1961)*

CAST

Clark Gable, Marilyn Monroe, Montgomery Clift, Thelma Ritter, Eli
Wallach, James Barton, Estelle Winwood, Kevin McCarthy, Dennis Shaw,
Philip Mitchell, Walter Ramage, Peggy Barton, J. Lewis Smith, Marietta
Tree, Bobby LaSalle, Ryall Bowker, Ralph Roberts.

CREDITS

Produced by Frank E. Taylor. Directed by John Huston. Screen play by
Arthur Miller. Photography by Russell Metty. Music by Alex North.
Edited by George Tomasini.

SYNOPSIS

Roslyn Tabor (Marilyn Monroe) divorces her husband, Raymond
(Kevin McCarthy), in Reno, Nevada. Through her landlady, Isabelle
Steers (Thelma Ritter), Roslyn meets Guido (Eli Wallach), an
ex-mechanic who has been a lost man since his wife's death. Guido is
attracted to her but when he introduces her to cowboy Gay Langland
(Clark Gable), the two fall in love.

Langland, a rugged individualist, plans to go after a herd of wild horses.

With Clark Gable

He teams up with Guido and Perce Howland (Montgomery Clift), a worn-out rodeo rider, for the roundup of these "misfits."

When Roslyn, who has come along, learns that the horses are to be slaughtered and converted into dog food, she tries to persuade Langland to call off the roundup. He flatly refuses. Later she appeals to equally tender-hearted Perce to release those horses that have been captured. When he does as she asks, Langland is furious and recaptures the leader of the horses after a rough-and-tumble struggle. Once he has demonstrated to all that he is the boss, he sets the horse free.

Financially, the roundup is a failure and the group splits up, but each has learned something from the ordeal. Langland and Roslyn, who have come to understand each other through the experience, make a new start together.

Marilyn's twenty-eighth film was her last completed motion picture. She had indeed come a long way. She had developed into a fine performer, and a continued unfolding of accomplishment appeared inevitable. Unfortunately two events marred her happiness—the death of her co-star, Clark Gable, and the end of her marriage to Arthur Miller, who had written the screen play for the film. Marilyn was badly shaken by both.

With Clark Gable and Montgomery Clift

With Estelle Winwood
and Clark Gable

With Montgomery Clift

Paul V. Beckley
in the *New York Herald Tribune:*

After the long drought of vital American pictures one can now cheer, for "The Misfits" is so distinctly American nobody but an American could have made it. To be honest, I'm not sure anybody could have made it except John Huston from an original script by Arthur Miller, and it is hard to believe Miller could have written it without Marilyn Monroe.

There are lines one feels Miss Monroe must have said on her own. . . . In this era when sex and violence are so exploited that our sensibilities are in danger of being dulled, here is a film in which both elements are as forceful as in life but never exploited for themselves. Here Miss Monroe is magic but not a living pin-up dangled in skin-tight satin before our eyes. . . . And can anyone deny that in this film these performers are at their best? You forget they are performing and feel that they "are."

Commenting further on this film in the "Lively Arts and Book Review" section of the Sunday New York Herald Tribune, February 5, 1961, Paul V. Beckley said:

There is much evidence in the picture that much of it has a personal relationship to Miss Monroe, but even so her performance ought to make those dubious of her acting ability reverse their opinions. Hers is a dramatic, serious, accurate performance; and Gable's, as I said in my review, is little less than great.

Kate Cameron
in the *New York Daily News:*

Gable has never done anything better on the screen, nor has Miss Monroe. Gable's acting is vibrant and lusty, hers true to the character as written by Miller. . . . The screen vibrates with emotion during the latter part of the film, as Marilyn and Gable engage in one of those battles of the sexes that seem eternal in their constant eruption. It is a poignant conflict between a man and a woman in love, with each trying to maintain individual characteristics and preserve a fundamental way of life.

Something's Got to Give

Twentieth Century-Fox

This would have been Marilyn's twenty-ninth picture. Only a few minutes of film with Marilyn were obtained. The director was George Cukor and Marilyn's co-stars were to have been Dean Martin, Cyd Charisse, Phil Silvers and Wally Cox. What footage Fox had of her was used in "Marilyn," which was a film history of the star's career with the studio. The screen play was later used as a Doris Day-James Garner vehicle and retitled "Move Over, Darling."

Marilyn died August 5, 1962.